We're all screwed up
(and that's ok)
By Dawn C. Walton

Dnuk

*Nothing needs to be the
way it's always been*

We're all screwed up (and that's ok)

Copyright © 2019 Dawn C. Walton

All rights reserved.

ISBN: 9781091952935

DEDICATION

This book is dedicated to my friends and family who put up with my constant Social Media updates about book progress, and willingly engage in brainstorming ideas for book names etc.

I also want to thank the hundreds of clients I have helped all over the world. They have taught me so much, and continue to amaze me with their determination and capacity to change. I think people are truly amazing.

More than anything this book is dedicated to my husband, Paul. His unerring belief in me has allowed me to be everything I am today.

We're all screwed up (and that's ok)

Introduction

It was my first day at University. I'd just moved into my room in the halls of residence that would be my home for the next academic year. In front of me, on a desk that was one of only three pieces of furniture in the room, I had placed a bottle of tablets. I had been diligently collecting the tablets for over a year. I had decided that if the first eighteen years of my life had been so horrible, I really didn't want to see the next eighteen, or the eighteen after that.

I looked out of the window at the people who walked by, each in their own world. Each oblivious to the choice I was about to make. It didn't make me feel alone. It made me feel untouchable. Nobody knew. Nobody cared. That was true freedom for me. Because my mother was disabled, my stepfather was her full-time carer. This meant there were always two people at home. I'd given a lot of thought to the best way to kill myself, and I was positive that I didn't want to be found and 'saved'. It wasn't a cry for help. It was a desire to no longer exist. My mother was on very strong painkillers for her disability, and had always warned me off her tablet drawer. Naturally, when I decided to kill myself, the easiest option was to collect the tablets that my mother had clearly told me would do the job. It was before tablets were packaged in foil bubble packs, so my mother didn't even notice one or two tablets disappearing every now and then. I didn't even try and take the tablets while I was at home. I planned, and waited until I was truly on my own, at University.

It didn't happen. I didn't kill myself. In fact, I didn't even take the lid off the bottle.

You may not have noticed before now, but all of us have multiple voices in our head all the time. Sometimes it's more obvious than others. For example, the voice that says you are going to start going to the gym, and the voice that snoozes the alarm because it's too early. Sometimes you think something and then tell yourself off for being so judgemental, convinced that the subject of your judgement can hear your thoughts. The reality is, lots of different versions of you share a space in your head. There is the son or daughter, partner, friend, work version and many more. Each of these parts has their own insecurities and their own strengths. I'm sure you are a very different version of you at work than you are when you are out with friends. Yet we barely notice these differences. We switch seamlessly between our different personalities, based on circumstances that are both external and internal.

These different parts can be quite subtle. In a 2018 study of 3000 UK adults, it was found that 62% of them had experienced imposter syndrome in the previous 12 months. Imposter Syndrome is where you believe you are not good enough to be doing what you do. It is a feeling that you do not belong. It is a constant worry that one day someone is going to call you out as not knowing enough to do your job, and you will get fired. Essentially, Imposter Syndrome is where a part of you feels inadequate, despite other parts of you getting on and doing the job. Even Michelle Obama, former first lady of the United States of America, has talked about having Imposter Syndrome.

Why am I talking about voices in my head and different parts of me at this point? Well I often wonder why I didn't open the bottle of tablets. All through my life I have hated myself. I have not lived. I have just survived. And yet, despite that, here I am now, writing this book.

It is my belief that one of the voices we all have in our head is what I refer to as "The Observer". The Observer is a relatively passive voice, compared to all the others that drive different behaviours. Even in the midst of turmoil, The Observer can offer commentary. I was once in a particularly tricky session with my therapist. At the time I was training to be a therapist myself, so sessions were always a combination of personal change, and observation of his technique. He had just taken me to a particularly traumatic memory, with the intent of transforming it. I was in the chair, physically shaking, surrounded by darkness, and then he said something that I found really interesting and clever. The Observer voice piped up with "Oooh I like the way he did that, it was really clever". Another voice replied with "Don't be ridiculous Dawn, you are in a terrible state here, you shouldn't be thinking about his therapy techniques". Meanwhile, another part of me was experiencing the trauma and working on the transformation.

At the time it seemed totally ridiculous to me to have those voices in my head. As time has passed, I have learned to accept that we are all made up of different parts, and that is normal and okay.

On that first day at University, it was the Observer that saved me. There was a part of me that wanted to die, but there was also a part of me that didn't feel like that was right. In the end, I went downstairs in the collection of flats that made up the halls of residence, and knocked on the doors of my fellow residents, introducing myself to them. This was totally uncharacteristic behaviour for me. I'd always been the person that sat quietly in a corner talking to no one. In that moment, I adopted a different persona. In many ways I did kill myself, but only the child part. That was the part that experienced abuse that was described by various people over the years as horrific. It was just that part of me I hated.

This new persona had a unique advantage. She had no limiting beliefs and no observable insecurities. She was confident, outgoing and sociable. Inside I was a mess. Everything was scary. Everything was unsafe. But I had learned to totally ignore that part of me.

This led to a very successful career and, in fact, life. At University I met the man I would eventually marry. I am still married to him now. He is my soul mate. He is the first person I ever spoke to openly about my childhood. He is the person who has always been there and always believed in me, unconditionally, despite all my flaws. I honestly believe that without his belief in me, I wouldn't be here now. I progressed rapidly through the ranks of the first company I worked for, and eventually ended up leaving a six-figure salary, and a senior executive role in a large Telecoms company, to become a full-time therapist in 2013.

I was successful because I was not restricted by the limiting beliefs that affected so many of the people I worked with. I remember when I first realised that other people didn't know what I was thinking. I was still in my early twenties when I was given the job of setting up a training department for the call centre where I was a technical support advisor. I had written the material, prepared the exercises and was all set up for my first workshop. There was no one observing me. My only audience was the eager trainees who had no idea how inexperienced I was. I was incredibly nervous. My mouth was dry, and I was physically shaking. However, I was a master of not letting people see how I was feeling. It had been a critical survival technique during my childhood and stood me in good stead in my working career (although it was not so good for personal relationships!).

The course went well, although I never really lost the nerves. I was waiting to be called out at any moment, expecting my students to point out that I didn't know what I was talking about. At the end of the workshop I handed out anonymous feedback forms and encouraged participants to give feedback on how I could improve the course. There was nothing on the forms. Every single one of the twenty students had given me full marks for content, delivery and pace. I was amazed and shocked. None of them knew. None of them could tell how nervous I was.

It was an important lesson for me and one that I still use to this day when I give talks. I don't worry about feeling nervous. I accept that there is a part of me that is worried about messing up, but it doesn't matter because no one else knows. No one can tell.

I have had a great life so far. At one point I was one of the world's foremost experts on call centres. I travelled the globe as a consultant, helping businesses improve. I lived and worked in many countries and connected with some of the most amazing people, many of whom I am still connected to as friends on Facebook. I have a brilliant circle of friends, both online and in person, that will seemingly do anything for me. My friends believe in me and hold me when I am having a wobble. They remind me how far I have come, and that I am capable of anything, even when I don't believe it myself. My husband and I have great fun and have each other's backs. My daughter is the funniest person I have ever met. She brings light and love into my life. The only time I have ever laughed until I cried has been around her. I have now, and always have had (as an adult), a huge amount of love and support in my life. If you read nothing else other than this paragraph then you would not be surprised, when you meet me, to see a confident, outgoing person who can deliver a talk and entertain hundreds of people.

In this book I will look at how, and why, we are all screwed up. You don't have to have had a terrible childhood to have a fear of public speaking or feel like you don't belong in a crowd of people. By the end of this book I want you to realise that being screwed up is normal, and that anything can change, if you want it to. Look around you today. Look at the people you know, and the people you don't know well. They are all screwed up. They all have their stuff going on in their heads. You know nothing about it. Despite their screw ups, they are all functioning perfectly well. We need to get over the idea that people with screw ups can't be normal, functioning members of society. Look at me. For most of my life I felt broken, anxious, depressed, suicidal. And yet, here I am, writing this book, helping others, with an amazing

We're all screwed up (and that's ok)

family, great friends and lots of happiness in my life.

We're all screwed up. That's perfectly okay. We still function.

The physical and mental aspects of the subconscious

Despite disagreement on percentages, it is generally accepted that the majority of brain activity happens outside of our conscious awareness. People tend to think there is a delineation between the mental and physical. This is not true. Everything can be either physical or mental

This is the point where I usually hear an argument that something like breaking a bone is very physical, and it's a bit crazy to call that a mental problem. Fine, let's talk about breaking a bone for a moment. Imagine you have broken a bone in your arm. The first thing you are likely to do is head to the Accident and Emergency department at your local hospital. You will go there so they can sort it out. But what do they actually do to fix the bone? Do they give you calcium supplements or injections to grow the bone back quicker? Do they inject a glue to stick it back together? No. In fact, a hospital does nothing to repair the bone. They might put a cast on the arm so that it doesn't heal crooked. They may even straighten it. But that's all they do. They line up your arm so that when your head heals the bone, it heals as it's supposed to be. You leave the hospital with your nice clean cast on. Over the next few weeks you get people to sign it and it gets more and more grubby. You struggle to shower and do all the things you normally do. It gets itchy, and inconvenient and soon the pain of the break is less of an issue than the discomfort of the cast. Then, 4-6 weeks later, you head back to the hospital or your doctor, so they can remove the cast. Magically, the bone has healed. You have done nothing. It's just healed. You attribute the healing to the cast and the doctors, but they've done nothing. This is not Harry Potter. This is not a magic potion or a spell. This has all happened outside your conscious awareness. This is your subconscious in action.

Now let's take it a step further. Let's say that you had an accident and your broken arm was only one of your injuries. You would notice that your body heals each injury slightly slower. Your subconscious has a finite capacity for healing. If it's healing a cut, it can't put as much focus on healing the bone. As a result, your broken arm will be slower to heal the more injuries you have. Not only does your mind heal your body, but it will heal more slowly when there are multiple injuries. As a logical leap, this must mean there is a speed control on healing. If it can heal slower, then if you can find a way, potentially it can heal faster. None of this is the due to the doctors. They, in the main, clear the way to give your mind and body connection the best chance. They put on a cast. They stitch open wounds. At best, they give you antibiotics to boost your body's ability to fight infection.

Everything has physical and mental elements. A broken arm is a physical injury with a mental component. Anxiety is a mental state with a physical component. So next time you say that an illness such as Chronic Fatigue Syndrome is a mental issue, and a broken bone is a physical issue, think again. Both have physical and mental components.

"I only need to run faster than you"

Two hikers are walking through the woods when a huge brown bear suddenly appears in the clearing about 50 feet in front of them. The bear sees the hikers and begins to head toward them. The first guy drops his backpack, digs out a pair of running shoes, and frantically begins to put them on. The second guy says, "What are you doing? Those shoes won't help you outrun that bear." "I don't need to outrun the bear," the first guy says. "I just need to outrun you."

The stress response has a very specific evolutionary purpose. It is a physical and emotional response designed to give you the best chance of surviving a predator attack. The mind and body automatically respond in a way that enables you to instantly fight, run away, or even stay totally still until the predator has gone away (Fight, Flight, Freeze). This is a complex process that doesn't rely on logic or situational analysis. The pre-frontal cortex, which is the thinking part of the brain, is disengaged before anything else happens. It's too slow. If you are being attacked by a sabre-toothed tiger and take a moment to examine your spear to see if it's suitable, and then your footwear to see if you can outrun it, it will have eaten you before you can act. As a result, the first thing that happens when faced with any sort of threat is that you go into an automatic survival state, where your pre-frontal cortex is disengaged, and your subconscious takes over. As well an emotional response, this response to feeling threatened is mostly physiological. These physiological adjustments are all designed to significantly increase your chances of surviving a life-threatening encounter with a predator.

Firstly, your heart rate increases, pumping blood around your body quicker, and increasing the flow of oxygen to your critical organs. At the same time, adrenaline and cortisol flood the body, activating a heightened state of alertness. Adrenaline serves multiple purposes. One lesser known function of adrenaline is that it suppresses viruses. If you are being attacked by a tiger and have to stop and ask it to give you a moment, because you have a rotten cold right now, well, you are not going to do very well! Also, the chance of a physical injury is a much more pressing issue than a virus. So instead of directing energy towards fighting viruses, your immune system is re-directed to be ready to fight infection from any injuries you might incur. While adrenaline is coursing through your blood, viruses are shoved out of the way and into the background. They are not destroyed, just kept at bay. This is why when you do a stressful job, you can often find that you get ill when you go on holiday. As the adrenaline subsides, the viruses barge back into your system and have their turn. This is also why, when I work with clients on traumatic issues from childhood, the first thing that sometimes happens after the session is they get ill. This can be a bit disturbing but is a good sign. It means the adrenaline has subsided. Once the suppressed viruses have cleared the system, they won't build up again.

Cortisol is also released. Like adrenaline, cortisol works with your blood to increase your survival chances. However, cortisol is designed as a more long-term solution. If you are in a perpetually unsafe environment, for example you are camped next to a pack of tigers, then cortisol will be released continuously. It will adjust the way you metabolise your food, to store fat around the organs that need it. If you suddenly need to engage fight, flight or freeze, then you will need instantly accessible energy. This is why the fat is stored around key organs, which also happen to be around your middle. This is also why weight tends to go on around the middle first.

Cortisol and adrenaline also serve to fight infection, directing your resources towards any injuries first, before other physical things are addressed. This has a knock-on effect on pain. If you are running, full pelt, from a tiger, and you stand on a sharp rock, then stopping to go "ouch, that hurts" will allow it to catch up with you and, you guessed it, you will die. Because of this, pain is adjusted by your subconscious according to the level of threat it perceives you to be under. The pain response is adjusted to ignore anything that may hinder survival, and to focus on those areas that need critical attention. This is why you often hear of amazing feats of strength, and of ignoring intense pain, from people who were in life-threatening situations. Adrenaline adjusts the normal physiological response.

None of this comes from the conscious mind. You don't have to activate a suit like Iron Man. It is a decision that is made by your subconscious when *it* perceives a threat. Not when *you* perceive a threat. It's an automated response that happens outside your conscious awareness and without you having to make a single choice.

I don't know about you, but I don't remember ever seeing a sabre-toothed tiger walking down the street. In fact, I don't remember seeing anything wandering around the streets that might pose a physical threat, in the same way as predators did in the caveman days. Yet I'm sure you can find plenty of examples where you have felt stressed, nervous, anxious or just out and out panicked. I certainly can. So how come we can all relate to this? The problem is that these days, your subconscious equates things that hurt you emotionally to things that used to hurt you physically. It triggers exactly the same response. As far as your brain is concerned, the fear you feel standing up in front of a room full of people is exactly the same as the fear you feel when facing down a predator.

Many people who struggle with anxiety, spend most of their time trying to override this unconscious response. This is where most of the problems come from. If your thinking brain has been switched off, how on earth are you going to think your way out of a protective response? This is even more of problem when the threat does not come from a specific event, such as having to do a presentation. When the fear comes from something generalised, like being around other people, then the stress response is activated, but never switched off. All the physiological changes that are designed to help you survive an immediate threat, remain activated long term. This throws your system off quite badly. It is not good to have a permanently increased heart rate. That is obvious. But what happens about the adrenaline response to ignoring viruses in favour of infections? What about the modified pain response? This is not part of the core design of your body. As a result, instead of doing one thing well, with great focus and intensity, your mind and body are thrown into chaos. Nothing is done well. Pain signals are confused. Viruses and infections are not given the level of attention they need. This is how problems that begin in the mind can lead to very significant physical issues.

If you want to address these issues, it is important to not simply focus on the physical or mental aspects, but to work holistically, considering the relationship between them.

Subconscious vs conscious

We hear a lot about living in the moment. Inspirational quotes say things like: "Don't look back, you are not going that way" or "When your past calls, don't answer. It has nothing to say". The problem is that most of the day you don't live in the moment. You are functioning on a form of autopilot. Just to show how this works, think about what you had for breakfast today.

There are a number of things that just happened without you having to cognitively engage with the question:

1. Your mind did an instant pattern match to the word breakfast. This is like a Google search, but way quicker. The search will have returned a match to the first meal of the day.
2. Armed with that fact, it will now search through your memories, moving back through time to whenever it was breakfast time, and zooming in on what you ate (or didn't eat).
3. Next the memory will be layered with meaning. Were you hungry? Did you enjoy it? How were you feeling at the

time? Your mind will be flooded with the meaning of the question "What did you have for breakfast?".

4. What happens next depends on what that meaning was. When I was a child I used to go and stay with my granny sometimes. She lived in the North Wales hills in an old farmhouse. My home life was not great. I had a stepmother that hated me and as a result I was badly neglected, and skeletally thin due to not being fed enough. We weren't poor. She just didn't care. When I went to my granny's to stay everything was different. There was so much delicious food. In the morning, breakfast was usually porridge covered in dark brown sugar and drizzled with evaporated milk. I used to stir it all in to create a wonderfully tasty and filling breakfast. So, when you ask me that question my brain has already accessed that memory. I have no choice in the matter.

All of these steps happen instantly, outside of your conscious awareness. The results are returned from the search in full 4D, with images, feelings, timings and other people, faster than you can do a google search on the word 'breakfast'. And you have no idea that all of this has just happened when you reply with "toast", or something else.

This is what normal looks like. This is what happens at least 90% of your day, probably more. Have you ever driven through a set of traffic lights and afterwards suddenly wondered whether they were actually green, or did you just run a red light? Or maybe you've driven from one place to another only to find, when you reach your destination, that you don't remember any of the journey. I've often done that and thought that I could have run someone over, and I probably wouldn't have even noticed.

We generally function perfectly well with our subconscious keeping things going, in a 'not-quite-present' state. But not all the time. Sometimes, the search that our subconscious executes when it is looking for a match in our memories, finds something that has a risk in it. If a situation reminds your subconscious of something that hurt you in the past, it will switch into a different state.

This state change begins with your cognitive function being disengaged. This function is used for problem solving and for rational and logical thought. If you are being attacked by a sabre-toothed tiger, and you take a moment to weigh up whether you have the right spear, or whether your footwear is suitable to outrun it, then chances are you are not going to live long enough to execute on your conclusions. While you are processing, the tiger is attacking and munching away on your legs. Your cognitive brain is simply too slow when you are faced with any sort of threat.

With your thinking brain disengaged, your subconscious is free to take control of your body and mind. It is an automatic response designed to give you the best chance of surviving an attack by a predator. You may know this as the fight or flight response. It also includes freeze, which is a more common response these days. You need to be able to either face up to the predator and win in a fight, run away faster than it runs without running out of energy, or be able to remain incredibly still for a lengthy period of time so that it loses track of you. This all happens automatically in response to your subconscious finding a match between something in your environment and a stored memory.

The most common phobia that tops the UK's list of top phobias is a fear of spiders. That means you either are somebody, or know somebody, that is scared of spiders. If you think of that person with a fear of spiders, whether it's you or someone else, when a spider comes into the room, they stop being themselves. They might scream or jump on a chair to escape. If you're not scared of spiders, you're there saying "You do know they can climb walls, right?". But they can't hear you. Their subconscious has disengaged the part of their brain that is capable of logic and understanding. They literally can't hear you when you tell them it can't hurt you or advise them calmly to put a glass over it or stand on it.

Then when the spider leaves the room, the subconscious allows you access to your prefrontal cortex again. You can once more look at the situation rationally. Now you feel like a muppet because you know the spider can't hurt you. Why on earth did you over-react like that? Well, don't worry. From now on you can say it's not you being crazy, it's your subconscious!

The thing about being scared of spiders is that most people aren't going to visit a therapist to help them overcome it. You just engineer your life around it. You make sure that you know which of your friends, or people close to you, is not scared of spiders, and call on them when necessary. I have a friend who spent two hours stuck in her bedroom once because there was a spider above the door. The spider didn't move for two hours, so neither did she! That's pretty screwed up, but she didn't get help for it. I was listening to the radio a couple of months ago and I heard a lady on the radio talking about a phobia that she had of Iced Gems. Iced Gems are small circular biscuit bases with a swirl of icing on top. Her phobia was so bad that she couldn't walk down the biscuit isle in the supermarket. That's where they may be lurking. She'd had the phobia for years, but never sought help. It's pretty screwed up. But we engineer our life around our screw ups.

Unfortunately, sometimes these screw ups are so pervasive that it's impossible to avoid them. For example, you might feel terrified at the prospect of being in the spotlight. When you are asked to speak in front of a room full of people, you panic. Your mouth goes dry. You lose the ability to think. You hate it. You try and avoid any situation where you might have to do it, but at work, it's almost impossible to avoid. It's also probably holding you back and stopping you applying for a job with more responsibility, because more responsibility often leads to more focus on you.

With this type of problem, you are likely to approach it in the same way as you might approach a fear of spiders (or biscuits!). You beat yourself up for being silly. You read lots of self-help books, attend workshops and courses, and try everything you can to sort your head out so you can think your way out of the problem. It doesn't work. Then you feel even more useless because you really should be able to sort this out.

"It's not you, It's me"

The problem with the way your subconscious operates is that it doesn't have any sort of quota. You can't say "You've already protected me from that spider today, you don't have to worry about me for the rest of the day". It is on alert all the time. For example, in a standard working day, every interaction could lead to feeling like you are being judged. Therefore, your subconscious barely has any need to re-engage your thinking brain.

These moments when your subconscious perceives a threat and takes over are what I refer to as 'alert points'. We all have our own individual and unique alert points, because they come from memories, and more specifically, from the meaning in the memories. By the time you are fourteen years old, you have experienced approximately 7,363,228 minutes. You are not going to remember every single one of these minutes. Even the human brain is not that powerful. There are different classifications of memory, including short and long term, sensory, episodic and autobiographical. For this book we will focus on autobiographical and episodic memory, as these memory types have the biggest impact on the things that screw you up.

The first type is Autobiographical memory. These are chronological memories, a bit like the old-fashioned photo albums, or photos on your phone, that are sorted in date order. Moments in time are stored in order, connected only by a sequence of time markers. Individual examples of that time are stored as snapshots. These are relatively two-dimensional memories without significance. I went to four different schools as I was growing up. If you asked me which schools I went to and when, I would start with the first, on Anglesey, then move to the second which was in Manchester. To do this I would visualise my first school, and some connected event from the second school. The third school was a primary school back on Anglesey. I am now thinking of the headmaster of that school and the house I lived in. From there I can make my way to the fourth school which was the last one

I went to. It's easy to approach this kind of autobiographical recollection. You simply pull on a thread and see where it leads you.

The second type of memory is Episodic. These are memories that are easy to recall because they have some sort of meaning. Unlike Autobiographical memories, they often appear unbidden.

Taking the example of my four schools, as I typed episodic memories were popping into my head.

My first school made me smile. I remembered the dinner ladies standing at a table with my brother and I after dinner time. The hall had no other kids there. They'd all gone out to play. The dinner ladies had put one of the giant metallic pots they used on the table. This one had custard in it. They were ladling a runny pale-yellow custard into our bowls, and we were hungrily polishing it off. I was starved as a child. My stepmother often neglected to feed us. Many years later I found out school knew all about this. So, the memory that I have just described made sense as the dinner ladies were doing their best to feed us up.

When I talked about my second school, I had a feeling of safety and fun. When I was about nine years old, I was living with my father and my stepmother. Life was full of fear and horror. I used to go and stay with my mother and her new man. When I was nine, I went to stay with my mother for the summer holidays, and at the end she didn't send me home. It was so exciting. We were fed and not hit. It seemed the days were bright and sunny. At the end of the road, was the primary school I went to. My brother, who was a little older, went to high school. My school had an amazing headmaster who put extra focus on developing kids with potential. I would get extra maths and English lessons and I loved them. I would run home after school, do my homework straight away and then read for the rest of the night. It was a wonderful time and, as I sit here typing this, I am smiling at the memory.

For the third school, everything goes dark. I am not totally sure what age I was when I moved back to Anglesey with my mother and stepfather, but I do know that everything changed. My stepfather was a tyrant, wielding emotional power over all of us, and treating me and my brother like his slaves. And then, after the sexual abuse started, he incorporated that into the threats and bullying. School, which had been a place to escape in Manchester, was now dull and boring. I was in a mixed age class because it was a small school. I wasn't learning anything. Up until then, school had always been the good place. Now it was grey and lonely.

I was in the third school for less than a year before I moved up to the last school. I don't have good or bad memories of this school. I went through most of this school in a daze. When I was around twelve, I told my mother that I was being abused. She was furious at me. I begged her to take me away from the situation, but she was too mad to listen. She told me that I should never talk about this again. I remember sitting on the bed in my room after that conversation feeling utterly hopeless. She didn't believe me. Maybe I was wrong. From that point onwards I have no memories. It is a total blank. I later learned that my subconscious has been protecting me from remembering what happened after that conversation with my mother. The memories are accessible to me again from the age of sixteen, when I had a conversation with my best friend that lifted the lid on what I had blocked out for the last four years. That is why, at eighteen years old, I was sitting in my University halls of residence, ready to kill myself. This means that I don't have autobiographical or episodic memories from when I was around twelve to sixteen years old. In fact, I recently reconnected with my best friend from that time. I cannot remember a single thing that we did together. Her name is Rebecca and I even had to ask her what I called her, as I genuinely had no idea.

It's a weird feeling, having a big blank space. I've spoken to quite a few people over the years, friends and clients, that say they don't remember much of their childhood. This is fairly normal. Even if you don't consciously remember, your subconscious has these episodic memories stored ready to call on at any moment. Very few people have a chunk that is fully locked away. I got so frustrated with not remembering even the good times, I arranged for a fellow therapist to help me find my way into that space. I knew the memories were there, just inaccessible. As we began to enter that blank space, I got a preview of what I was going to find. I quickly stopped what we were doing and said that I didn't need to go any further. I was happy to keep them locked away. In that brief moment, I realised that the abuse did not stop after I told my mother about it. That, combined with my mother telling me never to talk about it again, sent my subconscious into lockdown. Even now if I attempt to talk about some of what happened, I find myself unable to speak or move. It is how my subconscious protects me from entering memories that are so intensely painful, that they threaten my sanity.

Episodic memories are what your subconscious uses to create alert points. These memories carry an emotional meaning. That meaning is used by your subconscious to protect you once you are responsible for looking after yourself. This is usually after the age of sixteen. This means that generally, with the exception of trauma, the issues we face as adults come from lessons we learn as children.

They also form the basis of how we identify ourselves. You will have a narrative of what has happened in your life, that you use to project how you will react in different circumstances. Clients often say things like "This is what I always do when I'm in a relationship", or "I have always felt like that fat one", or "I have never felt good enough". Words like 'always' and 'never' are indicative of a narrative running in the background. Always has to start somewhere. When did you first learn that thing about yourself that now holds you back? Whilst it is relatively easy to change an episodic memory, changing the narrative is trickier as it requires evidence. Evidence can only be gathered by observing enough differences to prove the old narrative wrong. That takes time, and curiosity.

As you look back through my story of four schools, you can see that the range of emotion in episodic memories varies. Of the millions of moments you experience as you are growing up, meaning comes from small things, big things, sad things, happy things, and everything in between. Think about my story of breakfast. If I eat porridge with sugar on it, I am happy. Not because porridge is capable of making me happy, but because of the memory associated with eating porridge that pops into my head unbidden. If I'm feeling sad and lonely, I may now choose to eat something stodgy and satisfying like porridge. If I didn't do the job I do, I would have no idea that I was doing that. It would happen outside of my conscious awareness; instinctively I would turn to food for comfort.

Sometimes my clients say "I don't know if this really happened but...". You experience millions of moments as you grow up. There is no way your brain can remember everything that happens. It has to use some sort of algorithm to filter through what is important and only remember those things. What matters is what your subconscious perceives, not what you think, or want to remember. Any moment in time can be turned into an episodic memory. When a client is talking to me and a memory comes to mind, out of the millions of possible moments that could have popped up, there is always a reason. It is not your choice, nor is it anything to do with how good or bad your upbringing was. Another common thing for clients to say is, "I had a great childhood, I don't know what is wrong with me". You will be learning regardless, because finding meaning in moments when you are growing up, is critical to survival as an adult. This is a primitive thing. A baby animal needs to learn how to stay safe when it's sleeping or finding food. It will learn this when it is young, so that when it is older, it has the best chance of survival. Humans are the same. We learn as we grow up, so that we can stay safe as adults.

There is, of course, a catch with all of this. Recent research has shown that the prefrontal cortex part of the brain is not fully developed until you at least nineteen years old. This part of the brain is responsible for logical thought and reasoning. This means that your subconscious is observing, learning and locking in critical information about what hurts you, at an age where you lack the technical capacity to fully comprehend a situation. The younger you are when you learn the lesson, the less understanding you have, and the more skewed the meaning in the memory is likely to be.

The Amygdala is the first part of your brain to develop when you are a baby. This is the part of your brain that processes emotions. This means that you can experience something as a baby that is emotional, but you lack the words or imagery to express what that emotion is and where it comes from. The alert points are still established, but due to the lack of expression around them, they can end up with your subconscious being on permanent high alert "Just in case that thing happens".

By the time you are two years old you are beginning to learn how to express yourself and how to identify objects and actions. You are beginning to develop self-awareness. By five years old, children can look at themselves in a mirror and spot that a sticker is on their clothes rather than in the mirror. This increased awareness of self and your environment makes it a little easier for your subconscious to identify risks as you go through your day to day life. However, you still lack the ability to understand emotions. Your ability to understand anger and sadness and other emotions has not yet fully developed. You might understand that someone is shouting at you because they are angry, but you are unlikely, at this age, to understand why. How can you learn a lesson if you don't understand what the lesson is? But the lesson is still critical to survival. So, as with the earlier ages, the lesson you learn tends to be less specific. More general lessons risk incorporating things that are irrelevant. Think of it like fishing with a giant net. You can't be sure that you just catch fish. You are going to catch loads of unusable things from the sea, including bits of rubbish.

By the time you are seven years old, you are beginning to develop an awareness of how you fit in to the group. You are beginning to see the impact of your behaviour on others. Your level of self-awareness is increasing, and you are able to distinguish more complex emotions. You are able to identify the impact your behaviour might have on how other people feel. Because you understand more about the effect you have on other people, but still lack the cognitive development to fully understand actions and consequences, this is an age where people pleasing behaviour can really kick in. With my clients, this is particularly evident in the number of issues that are caused by things said by teachers when the client was at primary school (aged eleven and below). The lessons learned by the subconscious around this age tend to attempt to make sense of things you have got in trouble for, or were even unfairly accused of. In this situation the subconscious attempts to learn corrective actions to take in the future to avoid getting in trouble. Unfortunately, especially when unfairly accused of something, you are often not aware of exactly what you have done to get into trouble. As a result, you end up with a lesson similar to: 'I did something wrong and got in trouble. I don't know what I did wrong so I can't do something different on that thing. Therefore, I should watch out for everything I do because it could be wrong'. Then you are stuck with a lifetime of not feeling good enough, as your subconscious tries to second guess everything you do, to avoid getting into trouble.

By the time you are a teenager you are thinking about attraction and physical relationships. You are trying to look and behave in a way that makes you as attractive as possible. This is the primitive imperative to mate in action. Your brain has developed enough to understand body language and tone of voice. You have a clear identity and a high level of self-awareness. And, of course, you think you know everything! As your experiences of dealing with these complex emotions is limited, feelings can go from zero to maximum in no time at all. Your best friend going off with a different friend may feel like your world has fallen apart. For a subconscious that is looking for lessons about what hurts you, this high intensity emotional reaction cannot be ignored. Without the experience to tell you that you will be okay, or the resilience to let go of things that happen, the lesson is hard coded into your brain: you are not as good as everyone else. When the person you fancy takes more of an interest in your friend than you, this reinforces the belief. In many ways this period of your life is about consolidation. Evidence is gathered to validate the lessons you have already learned so that, by the time you are responsible for yourself and following these lessons, you have the best chance of surviving and not getting hurt.

Through all of these stages of development, your subconscious is learning and storing lessons from key moments. It is building a rule book of episodic memories that it can follow once you are an adult and responsible for yourself. By the time you are sixteen years old, your subconscious is in 'nodding head mode'. Each new meaningful moment is connected to the original lesson, further strengthening it for the next time it needs to be executed on.

We're all screwed up (and that's ok)

Because of how many millions of opportunities there are to learn and store these lessons as you grow up, it is feasible that you can go through your whole life without any of them being triggered. It is also possible that an event later in life can trigger one of these episodic memories, activating it. Once activated it will be added to the arsenal of alerts that your subconscious is looking out for. This can mean that things that used to be okay before the memory was activated, stop being okay after.

For example, a common phobia that I see clients for is a fear of flying. This more commonly relates to a fear of confined spaces, than a fear of actually being in an aeroplane. I have seen a number of clients who have flown very happily for most of their adult lives. Then one day, they took a flight with their children. It is generally true that an increased protective response is present once you become a parent. The flight with their children activated a lesson from when they were a child about confined spaces or being out of control. Whilst it is one thing to deal with that on your own, when you are responsible for the lives of small people, it becomes far more significant. After that first flight, even if they fly on their own, they still have the fear. It is hard to understand, but the solution is the same as if they had always had it;

we establish what episodic memory was linked to the fear and change the meaning. Without the meaning, it is no longer an alert point used by the subconscious to trigger a protective state. With their brain remaining engaged, they can think their way round the problem and dismiss the thoughts.

Even aside from your limited cognitive capacity as you learn, most of these lessons are a miscalculation, as they are based on the premise that the observed meaning carries with it a risk of being hurt. In a primitive subconscious, being hurt is a physical thing, and the biggest risk of physical hurt is death. After all, in the caveman days if you were injured by a predator you had little chance of survival. This means there are two fundamental flaws with this method of programming alert points.

Firstly, you are not dead. This may seem like a crazily obvious thing to say. However, your subconscious is trying to protect you from things that it believes could kill you. Those things never did kill you, so there is no merit in being on alert for them happening again.

Secondly, emotional hurt is not the same as physical hurt. It does not create physical injuries and it does not lead to death. However, your brain is incapable of distinguishing between physical hurt and emotional hurt, so triggers exactly the same protective response whatever the threat. This is why if you are afraid of standing up in front of a room full of people, you might feel the same level of physical and emotional panic as you would if I asked you to pop into the room next door and pet the wild tiger in there.

Sleep and reconsolidation theory

I have had a number of clients come to see me that are struggling with insomnia. This can be about the number of hours sleep they get in a night, and also the quality of sleep i.e. waking up through the night and struggling to get back to sleep. In brain function terms, sleep serves multiple purposes. In a standard eight-hour sleep cycle, you get two hours of REM sleep and six hours of deep, restorative sleep.

The deep sleep phase is triggered by the release of melatonin. This starts being naturally released by your brain at around 9pm, and ramps up to peak at around midnight. It then begins to tail off. This triggers a whole series of restorative processes within the body. I like to describe these as the night bugs. I imagine them being like those marketing items you get which are fluffy balls with googly eyes and a ribbon coming out with the company's logo or slogan on it. Your body is capable of remarkable healing in this phase of sleep. I tell my daughter that she needs to get sleep when she's ill, because the 'night bugs' need a chance to work and can't come out while she's awake.

The other thing that happens is the batteries in your brain are re-charged. The pre-frontal cortex part of your brain literally needs energy to function. This is why as you progress through your day, things that you planned on doing at the start of the say seem impossible by the end of it. Willpower and self-regulation are functions that require cognitive engagement. As you go through the day, you drain your cognitive batteries while you get stuff done. If the things you are doing require a large amount of cognitive override to achieve, then the batteries drain quicker.

Maybe you decide when you wake up that you are going to the gym after work. Going to the gym is intimidating for you. You feel that others will look at you and judge you for being overweight and unfit. In the morning you are determined to get on with the business of changing that. You have a long day at work with lots of demands. Before you even realise it, you are in front of the TV, with a glass of wine, eating whatever was easiest. Tomorrow, you tell yourself, tomorrow I will go to the gym. But the same thing happens again. You wake up, do a day's work, and end up back in front of the TV at the end of the day. You tell yourself this is a lack of motivation or laziness, but in reality, it is simply that willpower battery has run out of charge by the time you need it. If you like going to the gym, then a small amount of charge will be sufficient to provide motivation at the end of the day. If you don't, you'll find there is not enough.

This ratio of energy cost to achievement of tasks applies to anything. If the thing you want to do is loaded with meaning and consequences, then it will cost you a lot more of your precious cognitive resources to achieve it. This means that you will inevitably always run out by the end of the day. It might be doing your tax return, drinking less wine, eating less chocolate, exercising more, going out with your friends, applying for that job etc. Anything that requires you to overcome internal resistance will come at a higher cognitive resource cost.

This is a finite resource. Every night, when you sleep, the cognitive resource, or willpower pot, is recharged and refilled. The prefrontal cortex needs this energy to function effectively. Think of it like plugging your phone in to charge overnight. This means that your brain will last through the day. I'm sure, if you are like me, there have been occasions where you thought you had put your phone on to charge, only to find that you hadn't plugged it in properly. When this happens, I shut off all non-essential functions like WiFi and Bluetooth, so my phone will at least meet its core purpose of getting calls and checking emails. Your brain works the same way. If you do not get enough sleep at the right time, then the batteries are not fully recharged. The next day, you function on autopilot, but you are going to struggle to think straight. Decisions can seem impossible to make. Bad habits seem impossible to resist. Emotions might be a little more difficult to keep in check. We can function perfectly well in the trance state caused by a lack of sleep. But we can't achieve much that requires logic and rational thought. This is something often experienced by parents of young children. If you are a parent, you probably found that even though you knew you were sleep deprived, you constantly questioned why you couldn't do seemingly simple tasks, that you used to be able to do easily. I once put a DVD in the fridge in this state. I was putting my shopping away and had it in my hand with other stuff for the fridge. It took me days to find it!

This recharging of the cognitive batteries only happens in the deep sleep phase. This is why daytime naps do not make up for a lack of quality sleep at night. The release of melatonin is key. Daytime sleep tends to be more REM sleep. This is why it's not about how much sleep you get in hours, it's about when you get the sleep. This is also why it's more of a challenge for those who work shifts where they work through the night. The brain can adapt, but it's never quite as effective as night time sleep.

The first step to having more self-regulation and willpower is to ensure you get a good night's sleep. You can also do various things to change the rate at which you spend your cognitive resource. As mentioned, the more subconscious resistance there is to doing a task (or not doing it), the greater the cognitive cost to overcome it. If you remove the subconscious resistance, then the cognitive cost all goes down. You will see through the later chapters how you might be able to do that.

The second part of sleep is the REM (Rapid Eye Movement) sleep phase. While the deep sleep is restorative, the REM sleep is organisational. It usually happens before the melatonin kicks in. In this phase, your subconscious is doing the filing. It's taking everything that has happened in your day and trying to find the appropriate place to put it in the massive network of connections held in your memory. In computer terms (for the geeks among us) this is like the defrag process on the hard disk.

As you go through the day you are doing comparisons between what is happening and what you already know. This is a relatively passive process, in that so much information is bombarding you in every moment, that you only have time to compare now to some point in the past. You don't have the opportunity to update any of the memories or create new connections. That all happens at night, in the REM sleep phase. Your brain has so much information in it, that as you progress, there is little value in remembering everything that happens. In fact, there is not enough space to remember everything. This means that you only need to process stuff that has meaning. When you enter REM sleep your brain works its way through the events of the day. For each event, it looks for a match in your memory banks. Is there anything already there that today's event will add to or change? If a connection is found, your brain is physically updated to add the day's events to the chain of connected events. This is called reconsolidation theory and is an incredibly powerful and critical part of keeping your brain healthy. It is so effective, that it has been found that interfering with the REM sleep cycle deliberately, can be effective in changing the way traumatic memories are stored, helping remove the debilitating effects of Post Traumatic Stress Disorder (PTSD).

This is the simple, clean version of the process. What happens if your brain is not sure? What happens when the memory brought forward matches multiple significant memories? Or what if it is not clear where the day's event fits? In this situation the memory goes on a pile for processing later. When, during this phase, there are too many things that can't be processed, the REM sleep is extended, meaning the deep, restorative sleep phase is reduced. The restorative phase of sleep being reduced means that your cognitive batteries are not fully charged overnight. As a result, as you go through the following day, you are less likely to be able to process events with any level of rational thought. You then go into the following night's sleep cycle with even less clarity on how to process and reconcile events from through the day. In this way, a cycle is formed, of too little sleep, leading to challenging days, leading to too little sleep. When you can't process the events of the day, then you lose out on quality restorative sleep while your brain tries, and fails, to reconcile what is happening.

If you want to break this cycle, you need to sort the problems out through the day. If you are not triggered through the day, then when you reach the REM phase of the sleep cycle, your subconscious does not have such a large pile of paperwork to process. More things can be discarded. More things have an obvious link to previous experiences. The REM phase is shorter, leading to the deep sleep phase going back to normal. Your cognitive brain is now fully charged at the start of the day. As you progress through the day, you have more chance of dealing with events in a rational way. Emotion takes over less. As a result, you can go into the next night's REM phase with a head start. The cycle restores. Night problems come from the day. Sort the daytime stuff out and the night-time stuff will sort itself out.

The trouble with Tribbles

Everything that I have described here about the way the brain works is totally normal. Think about that for a moment. It is normal to be irrational. It is normal to be out of control of your choices. It is normal to continually go back to your past for evidence of the present and the future. It is normal to be screwed up. The challenges come from not realising that it's normal; from assuming that you can think your way past your problems.

There are three superpowers that people believe they have. These superpowers give the illusion of being in control of people and events. These superpowers don't actually exist, but the belief in them can act as the basis for problems you will experience in your lifetime.:

Superpower 1: Mind control.

You believe you can tell what people are thinking, and make them think things about you based on the way you behave

Superpower 2: Emotional manipulation.

You believe you have so much power that you can change the way people feel. You have enough control to make someone not love you, or love you.

Superpower 3: Time travel.

You believe you can revisit things you have done in the past, and replay them in a different way to change the outcome: "I should have...", "If only I hadn't".

For the next three chapters I am going to look at each of these superpowers in more detail, and help you to understand where they come from, and how a belief in them leads to being screwed up.

Mind Control Superpower

One of the most amazing superpowers that most people believe they have is the power to read minds. In fact, you probably go beyond that, and think that you have the ability to control minds. This may sound like something out of a Marvel film, rather than a day to day thing, but I can guarantee at some point in your life you have believed that your actions have changed the way someone treats you or thinks about you.

Let me ask you a question:

Have you ever walked into a room and worried what the people in there thought of you? I'm sure that you have.

Let me ask you a different question:

Do you think that you are that important, that when you walk into a room, people stop what they are doing and think about you?

This second question may seem ridiculous. However, both questions are asking the same thing.

The truth is no one knows what anyone else is thinking. At best, you can become adept at reading body language and get to know someone well enough to be reasonably accurate at interpreting their current mood. That doesn't mean you have any control over it. As you get to know someone better, you get better at reading their moods. You learn the typical way they might respond to different situations. You learn how far you can push them before they have a sense of humour failure. Still, no matter how well you know them, you can't actually read their thoughts.

A belief that you can read minds isn't the problem. The problem comes when you change the way you behave or look in response to what you think someone is thinking. This is when mind reading becomes unhelpful.

Let's say you are at work one day and you pass a colleague in the corridor. You smile at them and they don't smile back. They don't even make eye contact with you. You begin to wonder what is wrong with them. You look for an explanation of their behaviour by reviewing past interactions. Of course! There was that report that you were supposed to give them, but you've been swamped with loads of other stuff. If they had a problem, they should have just said instead of blanking you in the hallway. There is no justification for them treating you that way. They have no idea how much work you have to do. As you process the series of thoughts you find yourself getting quite mad with the colleague. Next time you see them you grumpily give them a copy of the report and stomp off. You don't see the confused look on their face. Because your colleague was probably just distracted. Maybe they were thinking about what they were going to have for dinner later, and how they needed to pop to the shops. Or maybe they were thinking of a conversation they had with their manager. You don't know what thoughts were behind their ignoring you. What you can be sure of is that it was nothing to do with you.

You think everyone thinks what you think

Because of the way the brain is structured, you are never really seeing things as they are. You are filtering everything through your database of memories. When a match is found with an episodic memory – a memory with meaning – you instantly gain a new filter that alters your perception of reality. When you first meet someone, you form an instant opinion of them based on this reality filter. If you have ever worried about your weight, then one of the first things you are likely to think is going to relate to the person's weight, and how their clothes look on them. If you have a thing about hair, you will notice their hair. If you have a thing about the shape of your nose, you will notice that first. If you worry about how you sound when you talk, you will notice their voice.

It is said that we form an impression of someone in the first six seconds. The first impression is based on your subconscious instantly accessing your database of memories and finding some sort of match to the person you have just met. What is talked about less is what happens after that six seconds. If you go into a bar and spot, across the room, a person who ticks all the boxes in terms of what you find attractive, you will have formed a first impression. If you then go and talk to them, and they come across as a total muppet, that first impression is no longer relevant. Equally you might meet someone that reminds you of someone you intensely dislike. When you first talk to that person, you enter into the conversation with all the prejudices from the match to your memories. These are usually outside of your conscious awareness. As the conversation progresses, reality will be increasingly incongruent with your memories, and the differences will soon outweigh the similarities. You will create new memories of this person. This is why I think it would be awful to be able to read minds. Imagine if you knew what everyone's initial unconscious thoughts were? You would really feel awful about yourself!

This is often the root of many of my clients problems. I had a client that believed his eyes gave away what he was thinking. It made him hyper aware of where he was looking. If I tell you not to notice where people are looking, what happens? You notice it right? In fact, it's really hard to stop noticing it. And because you notice it, you think everyone else is doing the same. This is all part of mind reading. Realising that it wasn't something anyone else paid attention to, allowed him to stop obsessing over where he looked in every conversation. I had another client that believed you should always learn a person's name, look them in the eyes and use their name when you met them. They believed it was a sign of disrespect when someone didn't do this. Because they believed it was important, then they expected that everyone must believe the same thing. Over the first five years of my business, I helped over seven hundred people. Some of these were local and some were online and therefore all over the world. I often cross paths with some of my local clients when I'm out and about. There is no way I am going to remember their name, especially outside of the context of my therapy room. I would rather not refer to them by name, than risk calling them the wrong name. To each of my clients they have had a unique and personal interaction with me. They are more likely to remember my name than I am to remember theirs. For this client, it would have been rude and disrespectful. For me it was the opposite. Realising that others may have different rules, and that their response was nothing to do with her, allowed her to let it go when people failed to respond as she'd like.

A few years ago, I was working on a programme run by a local charity that helped kids who were exposed to any sort of alcoholism. The programme was for fourteen to fifteen-year-old school girls and ran over ten weeks. At the start of the programme, the group leader drew a line on the floor. The girls were asked to stand on one side if they'd like to read minds, and the other side if they'd like to be invisible. At the start of the programme, almost all of the girls chose to be able to read minds. This is because they cared so much what others thought about them. The goal for the end of the programme was to get them to choose to stand on the other side and choose invisibility.

Once you realise that everyone is always thinking about themselves, and you have no control over that, it takes all the pressure off.

We're all screwed up (and that's ok)

You can be okay being you. Why is it that so many of us end up caring what others think? For many people, they are never happy with themselves. There is a term for allowing other people's opinions to inform your view of yourself: External Locus of Control (ELOC), or I always think of it as Ewok because Ewoks are kind of cute!. ELOC is where you allow the opinion of others to inform the way you see yourself. ELOC is not just about people that you have around you. I always thought that I didn't care what others thought about me. I was so absorbed in my own unhappy world, and I worked so hard at projecting a powerful f**k off shield to prevent people getting close, that I believed I was effectively invincible. When my therapist told me that I was in ELOC too much I scoffed at him, "I don't care what other people think", I said smugly. He went on to explain that ELOC is not just about the way you are affected by the opinions of people from your present life, but also by the people from your past. Having always felt that there was something wrong with me, based on the way the adults treated me as I grew up, I was indeed very affected by ELOC in that aspect.

The opposite of ELOC is Internal Locus of Control (ILOC). When in a state of ILOC you don't depend on anyone else to make you feel better about yourself. You recognise that everyone has their own screw ups and the way they behave has nothing to do with you. It is a state that I try and get my clients to, although very few can become fully ILOC. At the end of the day, it's in our core programming to fit in and feel like we belong to the pack. It's a very primitive, basic bit of programming. In the caveman days, it was not possible to survive on your own. A pack was critical for survival. The weakest person would be ousted from the pack. The strongest got the respect of the pack. These days it doesn't really matter if you have people around you. Everyone is capable of surviving on their own. By the way, surviving, and being happy, are very different things. You may be alive, but without human connection, most struggle to be happy. Despite the need for a pack not being relevant, most of us carry a core need to belong. A belief that you are different, that you don't fit in, and are weaker than others in some way, can lead to depression and even suicide.

According to the mental health charity The Samaritans, in the UK men are three times more likely to take their own lives than women. Suicide is the single biggest killer of men under the age of forty-five in the UK. When I look at stories of celebrities who have killed themselves, I see people who are outgoing, happy people, who clearly have a very different perception of reality to the people around them. Because they can't read minds but believe they can, they feel alone in their problems. They look around them thinking that they are the only one with their struggles. This chain of thoughts, without any reality check, leads to them taking their own lives.

It is the lack of reality check that causes the real problem. When you talk to people, and really listen, you will find that everyone is screwed up. Everyone has their own struggles. Everyone assumes that everyone else is fine. You believe their body language and outward behaviour, and you compare what you see to your internal story. The mismatch between what you believe and what you see causes most of the problems around self-esteem.

When I look at the ratio of male to female clients I see, only about a quarter of my clients are male. There is an obvious pattern that explains these low numbers. Men are less likely to talk. Why would men talking less be correlated with them being more likely to take their own lives? I had a client that I had been seeing occasionally for quite a while. Sometimes, I move into more of a coaching relationship with my clients. They use me to provide a safe, non-judgemental space to talk things through and gain focus. On one occasion, my client visited me for a chat as he was changing direction in his career, and needed some advice. He told me how he had been out for a beer with a good friend the night before, and mentioned how he was coming to see me. His friend was shocked, "You?" He said incredulously, "but you're so confident. Why on earth would you need to go and see someone?". As they talked the friend admitted that he had been taking anti-depressants for over ten years. They had never talked before. The friend felt it was only him. The friend believed what he thought he saw. Because men are less likely to talk, they are more likely to be consumed by their internal reality. They are more likely to believe that they are different and nobody else is struggling. That belief can lead to them feeling so isolated and so broken, that the only solution they can see is to end it. Yet all they need to do is talk. Talking would show them that others are also struggling. It would normalise the way they feel so that they can seek help to address it. They can say "This is my screw up right now", rather than "I am broken". Of course, women are guilty of this same thinking too, however they do tend to talk more. This means there is a bit of a reality check on this internal dialogue.

Nobody listens. Nobody cares.

If this is such a fundamental problem, why is it such a common thing for people to experience? It is part of our core programming to need to fit in, but why have we not evolved beyond it yet? In many ways, we have gone further the other way. It is now possible to feel bad about yourself with only the slightest gesture or observation from someone else. You don't need to be clouted over the head to know that someone doesn't like you (or does!). There are a couple of key periods or episodes in life that can lead to a heightened focus on what others think.

The first opportunity comes from an abusive childhood. In a 'normal' childhood, the consequence of doing something wrong is that you get a toy taken away, put in a timeout, or maybe you get a stern talking to. From that, you learn not to do the thing that has that consequence. It's a simple cause and effect; when I do this, then this happens. If there is a rule that you haven't learnt yet, for example, don't touch your father's laptop, then you learn it the first time you getting a telling off and you don't do it again. If you slip up, and do the same thing again, then the worst thing that happens is you get a slightly sterner talking to, or you lose a toy or treasured item for a bit longer than usual. This reinforces the equation, 'If I do this, then x happens", making it easier to avoid the same mistake in the future. This is how a regular childhood goes. You still learn things and attribute incorrect meaning to things, but you don't need to be totally in tune with the adults that care for you, in order to stay safe and learn those lessons.

When you have an abusive parent, that is either emotionally or physically abusive, or even a parent that has their own mental health problems that are visible and obvious, then these lessons and consequences are not quite so clear cut. There are two things that make the "If I do this, then X happens" rule harder to learn. The first is the condition "If I do this" and the second is the consequences "then x happens".

The first time I learned that it was not okay to get marks on my clothing was when my stepmother clouted me across the head at six years old. In that moment, after she had made clear why I was getting hit, I thought that I was going to be okay. I learned "If I stain my clothes, then I get hit". I became obsessive over trying to clean stains. No matter how hard I tried, I could not stop getting marks on my clothes. Therefore, the only option that remained for me was to try and clean the marks off, so she didn't notice. I really wish I had Google when I was growing up. There are solutions on there for getting every sort of stain out. I found that no matter how much I scrubbed with soap and the blue paper towels in the school toilets, I could not fully eradicate any stains. Instead I would try and fold my clothes or hold my arms in a way that it was not so obvious. I had also learned that I got beaten for breaking that particular rule. This was no timeout, or a firm telling off. Each time I learned a new lesson, the consequences were so severe, that I did everything in my power to make sure I didn't repeat the mistake.

This should have been enough. If there are clear actions and consequences, then as long as I follow the rule, I don't get hit again. Unfortunately, that was not true. It was not true because I wasn't really getting hit because I'd stained my clothes. I was getting hit because my stepmother hated me and was angry at me. In the "If I do this, then X happens" rule, I had learned about only one thing that I shouldn't do. It appears there were many more. The "If I do this…" part of the equation was impossible to learn. It became "Anything I do can mean there are consequences". The consequences were severe enough, that I would do everything I could to pre-empt them. If I just behaved really well and never did anything to upset her, then I would never get hit again. This is what I learned growing up with my stepmother. I learned to watch her. If she was in a bad mood, I could lie low and not get in trouble. If I was good and did everything she wanted, then I would not get hit. This is what I learned. But none of this was true.

The consequences of "If I do this, then X happens" are not always quite so severe or even so obvious. I have had various clients that have had a parent with really bad depression, suicidal tendencies or some form of psychosis. In these situations, the parent may spend time away in a mental institution. The family gets used to treading on eggshells around the parent, especially if there is a chance of them attempting to take their own life or being incarcerated in a mental hospital. These parents can be very needy, looking to everyone around them to make them feel better. I had one client whose mother would ask them how they looked, and then sob uncontrollably if they didn't like the answer. That's an awful lot to put on an eight-year-old child. Another client's mother would spend days in her room. They would give her meals and the rest of the time the whole family would tiptoe around. Looking at "If I do this, then X happens", the problem here is the lack of clarity around "If I do this...". What makes the parent worse? What makes them better?

Children growing up with abusive parents learn to watch like a hawk, for changes in mood or behaviour patterns. Whilst that is not great, in itself there is no harm in being more clued up to the impact you have on others. My daughter cannot tell when my husband has been pushed too far. My husband has a broken back and sometimes he may have twisted or stood on something which has increased his pain levels. When he's hurting, he tends to be less tolerant. I am used to watching and I can tell straight away when something is not right. I can tell when he's a bit more snappy than usual and know not to ask too much of him. My daughter, who has never had to worry about watching people, has no idea. It's not a lack of empathy. She can tell when someone is sad or upset, or angry. She just can't tell when her actions are pushing my husband too far.

All through her life, right from when she was very young, she has laughed in our faces when we have tried to tell her off or discipline her. She loved the naughty step or naughty spot. So much so, she'd take herself there for fun. She never had a strong attachment to any toys, so removing a toy did nothing. She knew we would never hurt her. In fairness, we couldn't even really be mad at her for any length of time because she was so funny, we'd just end up giggling. These days she isn't unruly and out of control. She's actually really good at taking herself out of a situation, thinking about it and apologising. Praise has always worked way better for her.

When I see my husband struggling, I try and warn her that now is not the time, but because she has no awareness of "If I do this, then X happens" in a bad way, she just keeps going. Then my husband snaps and shouts at her. When he does, a part of me shrivels up inside. My inner child wants to make everything okay and hide, both at the same time. My daughter usually just rolls her eyes and tells him off for being grumpy. Occasionally he shouts enough that she might cry after. The crying is due to shock as she had no idea he was about to shout at her. At no point, even when she is upset, have I ever seen her scared of him. She has absolutely no need to be.

It is a combination of watching for mood changes, and attempting to change behaviour to mitigate them, that leads a child to learn the illusion of control. It is this illusion of control over someone else's behaviour that can cause a problem long into their adult life. Sometimes, when I tell a client that it is an illusion, and they never really had any chance of affecting the way their parent behaved, they argue; "But it was! If I made him mad, he would beat me". Playing devil's advocate, let's assume it's true. Let us assume that as a child you were capable of watching your parent and behaving in such a way that you never triggered them. If that was true, then you would never have experienced any consequences of their behaviour. They would never have hit you again. They would never have locked themselves in their room. They would never have told you they didn't love you and that you were worthless. If it was true that you had power over them, then you'd be crazy to let them keep treating you in that way. You would simply exert your power and everything would be okay.

I can pretty much guarantee that if you had that kind of childhood, then you experienced the consequences of your parent's screw up on multiple occasions. You simply cannot say that you had power over the way they treated you, and you didn't have any power, at the same time. You either say you had power and you chose to let them abuse you, or, the real truth, which is it was nothing to do with you, and everything to do with them and their screw ups that made them treat you that way. You cannot read minds, and we are all screwed up. The way people treat you is nothing to do with you.

The problem is, children growing up in an environment like this become very adept at watching the adult closely. They are far more in tune to mood and changes in behaviour, than a child with a happy and safe upbringing. This carries through into their adult life. The illusion of power over how other people feel can lead to an overwhelming sense of responsibility for other people's actions and thoughts. The problem is that it is merely an illusion. When you feel responsible for others, it can lead to frustration at not being respected or paid attention to, and a feeling of failure as no matter what you do, nobody listens to you. It doesn't stop you trying though.

Over the years since I've been in practice, I have worked with a number of clients with a fear of death. If you think about it, there is nothing to fear from actually being dead. Dead is a state where you no longer exist. This means there has to be something more to a fear of death than simply being dead. You might assume that it would be a fear of the illness and pain that might lead to death, but this is not my experience of people with this fear. That would be a fear of illness, not a fear of death. In my experience, a fear of death comes from the perceived consequences for those left behind. It is usually a fear that is present in those with families. It comes from the deep sense of responsibility that the client holds for the well-being of everyone around them. This sense of responsibility comes from the illusion of control, learned as they grew up. In order to move beyond this fear, it is first necessary to help the client understand that they are not responsible for the feelings and behaviour of others. This is not an easy thing to let go of when it's been part of your whole life. It is also, not always a good thing to realise. If your it is not your purpose to make everyone happy, then who are you and what are you supposed to do? I have had some interesting 'discussions' with clients where they try to convince me that they really do have power over others. It is simply not true. Mind control is not a power that anyone possesses.

The second situation that leads to a belief in mind control happens in school. It starts from the age of seven or eight, and really kicks in between eleven and twelve years old. As discussed in the first chapter, this is the stage in development where children begin to develop a more sophisticated level of social awareness. How they compare to others, and their role in the group, becomes a keystone in how they know who they are. As everyone is in the same boat, the challenge is that everyone is watching everyone else's behaviour and trying to adapt to fit in. None of them can read minds, all of them have their own issues, and so what you have is a vicious circle where everyone is trying to be the same as everyone else.

When I did my Masters in Psychology, I decided to do my dissertation on the effect of episodic memories on problems experienced as adults. This was because my experience working with clients has demonstrated that most problems are founded on one or two significant memories from childhood. These aren't necessarily bad memories. They are just memories with a strong enough meaning to trigger the subconscious into action once they are older. As the dissertation would be run over only a few months, I needed to find a topic where data could be gathered quickly. I chose to look at a fear of public speaking. Glossophobia, or a fear of public speaking, is usually in the top five fears of any country. The prevalence of this fear would mean I could get plenty of data for analysis. I looked at the connection between the reason for the fear, which emotion was present, and a single childhood event where the same emotion was present. In an anonymous online survey, I asked about the emotion, and then, if they were to think of their earliest memory of feeling the same way, would it be before they were 5, between 5 and 10, or after they were 10. I then asked them to briefly describe the memory.

73% of the participants were able to identify a memory connected to the emotion they feel when speaking in front of people. Considering this was an online survey, with no prompting, this is a large number of participants. It shows how close to the surface these memories can be. Freud used to say stuff was buried deep. If it was buried, it would not affect your day to day life. These episodic memories are kept close to the surface so they are easily accessible if a risk of getting hurt is present. Of those who could access a connected memory, even more, 88%, had a memory that came from childhood. In summary, 88% of people who have a fear of public speaking have experienced something in their childhood that led to their fear.

I then analysed all the descriptions of the episodic memories to look for patterns. I was surprised to find that 69% of the childhood memories came from an experience at school, the majority before they were ten years old. The crazy thing is that these weren't big traumatic moments where a teacher, or other students, deliberately humiliated them. The memories were usually moments such as being asked a question they couldn't answer, or freezing when put on the spot. It's the internal interpretation of what that moment meant that turned it into a significant memory with meaning, not something bad and emotional that really happened.

Let's think about what we are really saying here. A high percentage of people experience anxiety when required to stand up in front of people and talk. Of those people, most have learnt this fear from a single, relatively insignificant moment that they experienced growing up. How crazy is that? One moment in time, a miscalculation of meaning of that moment, can lead to problems that you experience for the rest of your life! Even more crazy is that most of these misinterpretations are based on an assumption about what other people were thinking.

The thing about mind reading is that it leads you to worry too much what people think of you. Because of this, you often miss how screwed up and self-absorbed the people around you are. You spend so much time interpreting things as being about you, that you miss what is going on with them. Consider stereotypes. Stereotypes are just labels, that group people into common patterns of behaviour. These groupings emerge for a reason. Sometimes people label themselves, and join groups: people who knit, running clubs, gamers. The people in these clubs share common attributes, in general. This is how we interact as a society. Imagine you want to lose weight. The first thing you might do these days is look at what other people who want to lose weight have done. You may then join one or more groups of these people. Everyone in this group shares a common goal, but everyone's reasons for wanting to losing weight will be unique, as will yours. This is the way social groups work. They have certain generic profiles of people, and certain associated behaviours.

The school classroom also contains certain stereotypes. You may have missed these because it felt like the way you were treated at school was as a result of you, your behaviour, and your personal attributes and qualities. The reality is, you had nothing to do with the behaviour of the other kids in your class. If we replaced you with an android version, or a totally different kid, those around you would still have behaved in the same way. There are also stereotypical teachers in each school. I once did a talk to a local high school. I was talking to the twelve to fifteen-year-old students. When I discussed this with them, it was quite funny to see the murmurs travel through the kids as they identified the people in their class, and their school, that matched my descriptions. The roles I am describing can be taken up by a male or a female. They are not gender specific.

Every classroom has a class clown. This is a person that thrives on getting laughs out of their classmates. They will often disrupt the class to get the laughs. This disruption is sometimes welcome, and sometimes not, depending on the content of the lesson. It doesn't seem to matter how much trouble they get in, the class clown can't help themselves, they play up. They need others to laugh at them to feel like they fit in. To them, it doesn't matter whether their classmates are laughing at them, or with them. All that matters is that they are getting the attention. In my school this kid was called Grayson. My daughter is heading that way in her school. So far, she doesn't appear too disruptive with it, luckily. When she tells me how she has made her class laugh, her whole face lights up. As a point, the only time you can technically break into someone else's headspace is by making them laugh. Even then they need to find you funny. Making someone smile or laugh is the closest you will get to mind control. Nobody can get the class clown to stop. Even when the consequences outweigh the benefits, they will still play up, because they are working on the way they see the world. This has nothing to do with what anyone else actually thinks, and everything to do with their perception of what everyone thinks.

Every classroom has a sporty person. This person is either really good at one particular sport, or just a general all-rounder. They will play on the school team and this will give them a good status in the school, especially with a lot of the teachers. They will usually spend most of their time either playing their sport, or hanging around with the rest of the team members.

Every classroom has what we would call swots. They are the kid that always puts their hand up to answer the questions in class. They hand their homework in first and usually get good scores on tests and assignments. I was the swot in my class. I used to be in permanent competition with my best friend, Becky. When the teacher set us work to do in class, we would race to see which of us could finish it first, and then we'd ask for more work. It must have really annoyed our classmates, but we were oblivious to that.

A subset of the swots is the geeks. This group is ever changing as technology changes. When I was in school in the 80's computers were still quite new, so the kids that were into computers were a definite minority. As I write this book, everyone has a phone, and most kids have games consoles, so the geeks are not such a clear group any more. I used to hang out with other geek boys in the computer lab. Partly this was to escape rubbish weather at break times, but mostly it was because I was into computers. I am still a geek, using words like "sexy" to describe new technology. The geeks and swots are rarely well regarded by the other members of the class. They can lack communication and social skills, meaning they are often the first to be picked on in a class. Although this often leads them to feel isolated, there is sometimes more than one geek or swot in a class, so at least they have each other.

Every class also has a quiet person. They don't say much, or interact with people much. They keep their head below the parapet. This is a safe place to be. It is a place where you never have the attention of anyone. You are not significant enough for your classmates to pick on you. You never get singled out by teachers.

It was probably around this age that I developed my f**k off shield, without realising it. One of the most watched and shared TED talks of all time is the talk by Amy Cuddy on how you can use body language to feel confident. After doing a little research, she came up with the term 'power pose'. A power pose is a way of holding your body to change your physiology, leading to increased confidence. This is useful when you have to stand up and talk to people when you're feeling nervous. One such pose is to put your arms out as a 'Y'. This open gesture gives your lungs plenty of room to expand, allowing breath to flow easily. In many ways it's a vulnerable pose to be that open, but that actually sends a signal to the brain that you are safe and okay. Body language is powerful both internally and external for communicating signals. Closed body language, with arms folded and legs crossed, can send a signal to those around you that they should not come close. I clearly developed the ability to project subtle closed body language, without having to be as direct as holding my fingers up in the shape of a cross in front of me! The quite person in the class is closed down. They will rarely make eye contact with others. They will rarely speak out.

The most common thing that teachers used to write on my school report was that I was 'mature for my age'. I hated that. Of course, I was mature. Between the abuse and being a carer for my mother, I had not had a childhood. It's not normal to be mature for your age. Nor is it a compliment. I tell my daughter that she has to stay a kid. I get to be whatever age she is. If she grows up, then I have to grow up, and I'm not ready for that. I make a point to never tell her to act older or to grow up. The closest I get is to tell her off for acting like a three-year-old when she is actually ten.

Every class has a top dog or coolest kid. This is the person that looks like the most confident person out of everyone. Ironically, they are actually the most insecure person in a group. You see, the cool kid has a status, and the challenge with a status is that it needs work to maintain it. To be at the top of the tree, you need to make sure you are always higher up than everyone else. In school, maintaining this position usually involves pushing everyone down lower than you. As a result, the cool kid in the class is also often the bully. It is not good to be in a position where the only way you can ever feel good about yourself, is to make everyone else feel bad. At some point in your life you won't have enough people around you, or the people that are don't care what you think. When you have no one else to make you feel better, then all the insecurities that you have been working so hard to keep at bay are going to be exposed.

There have always been bullies and there has always been bullying. If you think back to your school experience, you will, I'm sure, be able to name your school bully. Many of you will also have experienced a period at school where you felt isolated and picked on. This may have been your whole time at school, or maybe it was just certain years at a certain school. Whichever, not many people get through school unscathed. For the purpose of this section, we are going to put physical bullying to one side. Bullying that involves physical violence has nothing to do with reading minds, although the trigger for it may well do. A bully picks on others to make themselves feel better. It is about status, which is why the cool kid can fall into this pattern of behaviour. Often the home life of the bully is such that they don't get a chance to be the most powerful one. It may be an abusive home, or they may even have lots of siblings so their voice doesn't get heard. Either way, at school they get the opportunity to take control back.

When you pick on someone, you have to have some framework for what you pick on them for. There are many things that you can choose: your physical look in terms of your size, skin colour, clothing, hair etc, your accent and voice, your mannerisms, the street you live in, how smart you are or how smart you are not. It is nothing to do with you what the bully chooses, and everything to do with them and the things that are important to them. It's as if they are looking at the world through their own personal Snapchat filter. It's hard to process this, because being picked on feels very personal. But it's only personal to the person doing the bullying. They will choose something that they have already been primed to notice, and they will criticise you for it irrespective of whether it is true or relevant. For example, if they are a redhead, they may be more likely to pick on someone for the colour of their hair. If they have been told they are fat by anyone in their life, they may pick on others about their size. I once had a young client who was getting bullied for a haircut that was very short. His bully called him 'baldy'. The client and I had a giggle about it because it seemed totally ridiculous that the only thing he could think of as an insult was the same as saying: "your hair, which will grow back, is quite short just now".

Bullying is a power play and, crazy though this may seem, all the power sits with the person being picked on. Without you, the bully is nothing. There is no fun in calling out insults to thin air. They need a reaction to make themselves feel better. I always think that's such a shame. What a terrible place to be where the only way you can feel okay about yourself is to make someone else feel bad. This is almost impossible for you to realise at the time it's happening unfortunately. At a time where you are struggling to fit in, once you hit puberty and that becomes the overriding drive, someone starts repeatedly undermining you and forcing you to focus on comparing your personal qualities and physical attributes to everyone around you. You were already primed to think about it anyway, and this person doesn't allow you any respite. Your filter on the world becomes permanently tainted with this way of seeing things.

Try something for me. Name two things that you don't particularly like about yourself. Now name two things that you think are brilliant about yourself. Which of those two questions did you find easiest to answer? I suspect the former.

The biggest bully in my school was a girl called Lisa. Everyone knew she was the one to be avoided. She had a relatively small pack of two or three friends. I never had any problem with bullying at school. I spent very little time actually in the present. I was just in a world of darkness in my head. It would take a seriously powerful person to get anywhere near that internal world. It's entirely possible that I was bullied, I just didn't notice it! I do remember a run in with Lisa once. I was standing at the top of two flights of stairs, waiting to go into the computer lab where I spent most of my breaks. Initially this was in a separate building we called the 'old school'. There weren't many classes and it was supposedly off-limits during break. The exception was those of us who were allowed in to use the computers. Lisa and her cronies appeared at the bottom of the stairs and she yelled something threatening up at me. There was a brief exchange of words in which I vaguely remember her threatening to come upstairs and beat me up. I wish I could remember what I said, because whatever it was resulted in me 'winning' the exchange and she and her cronies wandered off, leaving me alone. I couldn't believe my luck.

Like everyone I was scared of Lisa. There was a boy on the school bus that she relentlessly picked on. This lad was the same age as her. He wasn't a victim type at all. I think he was on the rugby team, her equal in size and build. He was a popular lad with a good collection of friends. One particular day she was so relentless, picking on him verbally and physically by twisting his ear, he actually ended up in tears. Buses are a weird sort of dead zone when it comes to rules and behaviour control. Technically, on the bus, you are neither under school governance, nor the responsibility of your parents. My school bus journey was around an hour. Anything could go on in that time. What amazed me is that the boy in question didn't retaliate. He just let her do anything she wanted to him. To this day I can't decide if that was admirable or daft.

There is a lot of talk about bullying and trolling on Social Media at the moment. The bullying on Social Media is no different from the nature of what happens in the classroom. The problem is, you used to be able to go home, and leave the environment where you were being picked on. Now it is unrelenting. Even when you are at home, they are all there. In addition, if you call someone a name or insult them, it disappears when spoken. On Social Media it is a permanent record that can be shared with other people, that weren't even part of the conversation. If you talk about someone, they can get to see it. And the reach is far wider. If you have that kid in your class that is a problem, then your class knows about it but nobody else. Because of Social Media, the whole school can now find out. This lack of ability to escape to a safe place, the permanence of what is said, and the reach beyond your immediate circle, is what makes bullying on Social Media such a big issue.

The other problem with the online world is the anonymous nature of commenting. When people make nasty comments anonymously, this is called Trolling. To understand how easy it is to become a Troll, imagine that you have an invisibility cloak, like in the Harry Potter films. You walk into a huge hall filled with people, none of whom can see you. What would you do differently? Would you do anything that you wouldn't do if they could see you? Maybe you'd listen in on a conversation. Maybe you would move a chair and try and freak them out. Would you worry what they thought about you when they can't even see you? I suspect not. This is how it feels to comment on stuff online. You can do it with no repercussions. This is why the actions of large Social Media providers tend to focus around removing anonymity.

When I talk to my daughter about online communication, I make clear that you should never share anything that you are not willing for the whole world to see. It doesn't matter whether you think they will or not, if you can't say "I'd be happy for anyone to see or hear this" then you should not take a photo or make a comment.

Every cool kid has a pack. These are kids that hang out with the cool kid because they also want to seem cool, and it's easier to gain that through association than do it themselves. However, sometimes they also hang out with the cool kid so they don't get picked on. The friendships in these groups can seem enviable. Any friendship that is based on fear and intimidation is not really a good friendship, in my opinion. I think a friend is someone that has your back no matter what. You may not always like them, and you may not always get on particularly well, but you believe in each other and forgive each other. A friendship with a kid with significant self-confidence issues means that they will not accept anyone looking better than them. Far from building you up, they are likely to do the opposite. The thing with being part of a pack is you are often oblivious to the impact of your behaviour on those around you, because you are in a permanent state of high alert. You need to make sure, more than with others, that you don't lose status and fall out of the pack. As with the cool kid/bully, if you need someone else to make you feel ok about yourself then you are always going to have a problem. Besides, in any group of kids, there is usually one that is the underdog and so still gets picked on.

I moved village, but not school, when I was around fourteen years old. This meant I took a different bus to school. I had two other friends that lived in the same village and travelled on the same bus. One was the same age and the other a year younger. I was great friends with both of these girls. They were very different people and when I hung out with each individually, we had a good time, even despite my inner turmoil and inner focus. They would also hang out with each other quite often and that worked fine. However, when we travelled on the bus together it was always a different story. For some reason, the three of us being together fundamentally altered the dynamics and always left one feeling isolated. There was one particular bus journey where I inadvertently reduced my best friend, the one that was the same age as me, to tears. It was not intentional. I can't remember what I said. What I can remember is that I felt so bad after, that I would have happily allowed her and anyone to physically beat the heck out of me. I wanted to hurt externally because I hurt so much internally. As I type, while the emotion is not as strong, it is still very much present. This incident happened thirty years ago, and yet I still feel bad for making my friend cry. I had been hurt so much in my life up until that point, that the thought of hurting someone else was almost intolerable. I don't know if my friend remembers that moment. She may or may not. On the scale of things that she was dealing with, which included her mum dying (or being ill depending on when it was), this was probably relatively insignificant. However, I have never been able to read minds. I had no idea at the time that it wasn't up to me how she took my words. I would never say anything that made her cry on purpose. So why did I feel so responsible? It's because we all innately believe we have control over what others think of us, and how they react to what we say and do. This is simply not true.

As you think back to your own experiences in school, and the classroom dynamics, if you are struggling to remember who filled the stereotype of each kid in your class, it probably means it was you!

There is also a common dynamic of behaviours among teachers. Every school has a teacher that wants to be seen as cool and down with the kids. Every school has a teacher that has no confidence and self-esteem. This teacher struggles to control the class. In fact, they are the one the class clown usually has the most fun with. Every school has a teacher that is really grumpy and strict. And every school has a teacher that is really good. It's not relevant what the subject is, they are just good at teaching. If you can think of who this teacher was for you, throughout your entire school years, then what it means is no matter what your academic tendencies, anything you have struggled with was because you weren't being taught correctly. If there was even one teacher that you could learn from, then it was never about your abilities, and all about the way you were taught.

The misguided belief in mind reading, and the need to fit in, means that few people realise how differently boys and girls think, particular once they reach puberty. This way of thinking varies slightly in same sex relationships, so consider the following section as being applicable predominantly to heterosexual relationships.

From the age of eleven onwards, boys become almost entirely focussed on getting off with girls. There is not a huge amount of sophistication involved in this process. No complex thought process and planning. It tends to rely on the boy making himself more attractive, in comparison to the other boys. The definition of attractiveness is what varies quite a lot between boys and girls. For boys it is a very primitive approach based on what made a caveman attractive! As a result, the boys begin to compete with each other, often resulting in idiotic behaviour, in an attempt to make the other boys see them as the top dog. Actions that make the other boys laugh or look up to them in admiration all count towards making them the top dog in the pack. Ironically, the girls often become the victims of these attempts. It is not uncommon for boys to tease girls for having bigger breasts, or no breasts. I have had clients who have had their self-esteem destroyed from being relentlessly teased at school by boys about the size of their breasts. And yet, as adults, this can become a much sought-after physical trait!

For a girl, the definition of attractiveness is a very different thing. Girls live in their heads. They have worlds and stories planned. By the time my daughter was eight she'd planned that, with her future husband, they would have two children. She had already picked out their names and planned to stay at home while her husband went out to work. I honestly could not understand how she was my daughter sometimes as this was nothing I had ever even remotely talked about as a life plan! Girls interpret everything in comparison to the alternative reality they hold in their head. "He talked to my best friend and smiled at her, he must like her more than me. The cow! How dare she steal him from me. She knows he's mine", and thoughts like that are commonplace in a girl's head. Nobody else has any clue what they are thinking until one day some poor boy is blindsided when the girl offloads onto him a catalogue of the misdemeanours he has been guilty of over the last few months. The poor boy is unlikely to have had any forewarning of the impact of their behaviours. In fact, they are unlikely to even recognise that they were responsible for the behaviours they are being accused of. The problem is not just that girls have these complex virtual realities constructed in their brain, but also that they don't ever talk to anyone about what they are. They just assume everyone sees things the same way as them. They can interpret something, carry a grudge about it, and fall out with someone, based on absolutely nothing.

I spend a lot of time and effort repeatedly reinforcing to my daughter that she can't read minds. I jump on every opportunity to highlight examples of misinterpretation, from text messages, to TV shows. I guess that is what Shakespeare did so well in all of his plays. The consequences of overhearing and misinterpreting are rife in his plays, with often lethal consequences. It's just a shame they are so unrelatable to modern kids. The concepts are sound, even if the setting needs to vary.

A short while ago I took my daughter swimming with her best friend and her mother, who is a good friend of mine. We had a great hour or so in the pool of a private club, and then went for dinner in the bar afterwards. We sat at a table that had a sofa and two comfy chairs. My friend and I took the comfy chairs and the girls shared the sofa. Both girls spent the meal curled up, not talking to each other. When I got back to the car, I asked my daughter what was wrong. She initially didn't want to talk about it, but soon burst into tears saying her best friend was so much prettier than her, and much more popular than her, and better at everything at school whereas she always messed all her friendships and was ugly. I had no idea where this all came from, but did what I always do and pointed out that she can't read minds, pointed out some of her good qualities, and highlighted some of her friend's insecurities. I also reminded her that if you need someone else to make you feel good about yourself then you will always be screwed up. I got her calmed down and then we drove home. When I got home, I got a message from her friend's mother asking if she was okay. I explained what she had told me. The mother laughed and replied that her daughter had just had the same meltdown about my daughter. I laughed so much and showed the message to my daughter, instructing her in the future to just talk to her friend, and not hold all these crazy ideas in her head.

I would like to say that was the end of it, but I've had countless other similar conversations over the last few years, nudging her all the time away from needing to worry what others think. It's an uphill battle as I'm constantly working against her programming.

The challenge is you are fighting your core programming to ignore the need to fit in. This means you are more likely to interpret situations as being in your control. There are a few shifts in perception that can help you work around this. You can find a couple of strategies in the self-help section at the end of this book.

The important thing to remember is that nobody is thinking about you. Essentially nobody cares what you do or what you are thinking. This is not in a nasty way. It's just that everyone is too self-absorbed. You can only relate to the world based on your own experiences and so we are all innately selfish

Try this. I am going to tell you something and I want you to be very aware of the first thing that pops into your mind.

I like coffee and my favourite is a Starbucks latte.

What did you think? Maybe you thought about whether you like coffee or not. Maybe you agree and like Starbucks or maybe another coffee provider is your favourite. Maybe you are vegan and don't drink milk. Or maybe you hate milk. I can pretty much guarantee that you weren't thinking about the first 2 words in my sentence. The fact that "I like" it became instantly irrelevant as you processed my sentence and worked out what it meant to you.

Nobody listens to hear. People listen to answer. Every conversation is like a game of tennis. I say something. You hear it and your brain searches for a match that gives some sort of meaning to what I have said, based on your own experiences and memories. You then reply, based on what it means to you. I do the same. And so it goes, that most conversations involve two people speaking their thoughts, without every truly listening to what the other person says.

I used to think I was a horrible person. I really wanted to be able to help my friends. I wanted to be the person they came to when they were struggling. Yet they never spoke to me. I would see them struggle and talk to their other friends. I felt like such a rubbish person that no one trusted me. As things changed for me, I became less internally focussed. I began to listen to hear, instead of listening to answer. I stopped making everything about me. Miraculously, my friends started opening up and sharing. I guess it must have been really frustrating to have me react badly every time they told me something. It was one of the biggest challenges during my early days as a therapist, to learn to listen instead of constantly pattern matching to my own experiences. It's really hard when there is a high probability you have experienced something similar to a client. My brain naturally presented me with matching experiences. This is not helpful in therapy. My model of the world has nothing to do with the way the client sees things, and what works for me is unlikely to work for them. For me, therapy is about working with the way my client sees things and shifting that perception. I learnt how to do this over time. It is far less taxing too, as I don't trigger the emotions associated with the memories in the way I used to.

At the end of the day, in the nicest possible way, nobody cares. Everybody is thinking about themselves. Nobody is thinking about you, not even the person that is closest to you. Watch people. Notice how people listen to answer, not to hear. Notice how obvious it is how screwed up people are when you are no longer worried what they think of you.

Emotional Control Superpower

When a baby animal is born, it needs to form a bond with its mother. If it fails to do this, then it has no chance of surviving. This means babies are genetically imprinted with a need to connect. Whilst evolution means that humans don't instantly die if they fail to bond, we retain the genetic coding that drives the need for connection. As we have evolved, this core need to bond has evolved into a broader spectrum need to be responsible for other people's feelings, particularly love. Not only is the mother a key player in this need, but also any responsible carer; so, fathers, grandparents, uncles and aunties can all be significant in reinforcing this belief.

The biggest cause of problems in the majority of my clients, is a belief that they are not loveable. This is what I would refer to as an identity level belief. It's not something they did, or didn't do, that caused it. It was their very existence that was not good enough. How do you escape from that? How do you learn from that and protect yourself from it? The answer is you can't.

However, there is one thing that you will know with certainty if you are a parent: there is nothing that your child could do that will change how you feel about them. You will love them no matter what they do. Additionally, there is nothing you ever do or say that implies you don't love them. You may not like them very much sometimes, but you still love them! When talking parental love, if you love someone you love them no matter what they do and no matter what you do. Note that if you don't love someone, you don't love them no matter what they do and no matter what you do. Love and behaviour are not connected. This means that when working with a client I don't need to prove whether they were loved or not. That is irrelevant. I just need to help them see that it's irrelevant to them too. They have no power to change how someone else feels, and they have no responsibility for other people's feeling.

The problem with the subconscious being on alert all the time, is that you can find emotions taking over without any conscious control. If you find yourself in a negative emotional state, you can't consciously think your way out of it. As discussed in an earlier chapter, your thinking brain has been disengaged as soon as the emotions take over. You will often find schools using anger scales for the children. The idea is for them to take a different action depending on how close to anger they are. This should allow them to stop before it goes too far. However, an anger scale is a conscious task, and by the time they look at the scale they have probably already lost their conscious control.

The only way out of a negative emotional state, is to replace it with a positive emotional state. That way you get your thinking brain back and you can start making better choices. Have you ever heard a song on the radio that evoked a memory with a strong emotion attached? Even after the song has finished playing, the emotion lingers. This is an anchor. Anchors can trigger positive or negative emotions by matching to episodic memories with the same emotion. Instead of thinking your way out of the negative emotional state, you can deliberately trigger a positive emotion, disengage the subconscious, and regain the ability to think. There is a technique in the self-help section of this book which you can use to build your own positive anchor.

If it is true that your negative emotional states are triggered by an anchor that activates an episodic memory, then the same is true for everyone else. This means that there is no way you can know what emotional triggers other people have. If you can't know, how can you possibly be responsible for the way other people feel? Like mind control, a belief in emotional control is linked to your perception that you know what is going on in someone else's head. We have already established that you are not present most of the time. You are subject to your autobiographical and episodic memories. Episodic memories are those with meaning, which means they usually have both a lesson and an emotion attached. This emotion is used by the subconscious as a trigger to a protective state. For example, if someone at work criticises something you did, making you feel like you are not good enough, that feeling can trigger an episodic memory match where your teacher criticised something you did in class. Your thinking brain is then disengaged, and the emotion takes over as you enter a protective state. Emotions are not logical. You cannot choose to ignore them. No one else could know that you had a memory where a teacher made you feel bad. You can't put the responsibility on the work colleague for making you feel bad. If they knew the significance, they might have tried to phrase it a different way to make it less emotional. The problem is, that they didn't know, and you probably don't realise that it's triggering that particular memory.

A lack of ability to read minds, means it is almost impossible to deliberately trigger an emotional state in someone. You have no idea what another person has in their database of episodic memories. Even when you are very close to someone, you may have learned what triggers them, but you may not know why. Most people do not deliberately trigger people they care about. It's also almost impossible to change someone's emotional state, even if you recognise what state they are in (which is unlikely). You need to find the correct corresponding positive emotion. Emotions come from inside, not from external sources. This mean you have no responsibility for creating feelings in others or changing them. It's a lesson that most people with an abusive childhood struggle to learn. When you have been hurt yourself, the thought of causing that kind of hurt in someone else is abhorrent.

Looking back on my childhood I can now say that I was really unlucky. I like to yell plot twist randomly as I tell my story, because it just seems like if something could go wrong it did. I don't have anyone to ask about exact timelines, and I don't have any photos to look back on, but from what I can tell everything was fine until I was about six years old. Up until that age I was living with my mother and father. When I was around six, my mother left the house to go and live with another man. She took my brother and I with her. I don't know exactly what happened over that period, but I know that the relationship was not going well, and my father fetched us back to North Wales and was given custody of us. As this was in the seventies, I can be sure it would take a lot for the courts to give custody to the father, so I know something had gone on.

My father soon remarried. The woman who became my stepmother was a close family friend. We lived in a cottage on a farm and my father was the manager, so he was rarely in the house. This left my stepmother as a responsible carer. My stepmother hated us. I have heard stories of why this was and what her issues were, but they are not mine to tell. I can only tell you what I experienced. One day, when I was around six, I came home from school only to find myself in trouble. I was standing in a porch area that had been built on the edge of the cottage. My brother was next to me. We'd been dropped off by the taxi that took us to and from school. My stepmother had noticed a stain on my white top. In that moment I learnt that one of the things we weren't allowed to do was get our clothes dirty. I learned this lesson by receiving a sharp, hard slap across my head. It was a such a shock, that I remember it very clearly to this day. I was hit many, many more times after that but I don't consciously remember most of them, as they didn't have the meaning associated with that first one.

I learned that the consequence for doing things wrong was to be hit. The challenge when you are a child is that you are still learning what is and isn't ok. If you get hit randomly, then you have no chance of working out what you can and can't do. I knew that crying wasn't okay, because one night when I was crying because I heard my father and stepmother arguing, she came in and threatened to hit me if I didn't stop crying. Now I knew: don't get dirty, don't cry or make a fuss; the rules kept building. Nothing I did was right.

As well as directly taking her anger out on us, she also neglected us. We were starved. This was not because we were poor. It was because she didn't care about looking after us. On weekends and school holidays we were sent outside and not allowed back in the house all day. If the weather was bad, we were seated in the living room with the TV on. We weren't allowed to move or change the channel.

Growing up with my stepmother, I believed that if I just behaved in a way that didn't annoy her, then she would like me. I believed that my behaviour could stop her getting angry. This was the first step in learning that I was responsible for how others felt. It is a fundamental belief that I still struggle with to this day. When something triggers me into a protective state, the first outward indication of this is that I begin to apologise for everything I do. I take it very personally when someone gets upset in response to something I say or do, and dig out a metaphorical "spiky stick" to whip myself with. Bad Dawn, you hurt them.

The only escape we had from my stepmother was when we went to stay with my granny. She was a lovely lady. She had a dog that she used to take on long walks every day. She lived on the Lleyn Peninsula in North Wales so the walks were always through stunning landscapes. My mother said she wasn't a great cook, but I thought she was amazing. After all, we were used to not getting fed. My granny gave us porridge with dark brown sugar and evaporated milk, toasted crumpets on the fire, and generally fed us up nicely. We didn't go often but I remember many more things from my time with her than I do my time growing up with my father and stepmother.

To get to my granny's house, we had to go with my grandfather. He drove a large white transit van that stank of fish, because he spent most of his time out on the trawler fishing. My brother used to make me sit next to my grandfather for the hour-long trip. Neither of us wanted to sit next to him. He used to put his hand down my pants while he was driving. I was too young to know what he was doing, I just knew it was uncomfortable and I didn't like it, but my brother was older than me so I had no choice but to take the middle seat. I am pretty sure other stuff went on with him, but I don't remember it. It paled into insignificance in comparison with the stuff that happened later! As with the neglect and abuse from my stepmother, I later learned that everyone knew my grandfather was a paedophile and yet no one protected me from him. I told my mother about him exposing himself to me once, and she said she acted on it, but there are no records.

I hope you are keeping count? We are now up to three adults that either directly abused me, or did nothing to protect me.

When I was around eight years old a lady came to visit us. By this point my mother was back in my life. My brother and I had been to stay with her and her new man over a few school holidays. These had been good times. We had been fed, and we weren't hit. By that stage, I had a very simple definition of what was good!

We're all screwed up (and that's ok)

We didn't know this woman was from Social services. We were strictly briefed by my stepmother to tell the lady, when asked, that we wanted to remain living with my father and stepmother. I find this hard to understand when I look back. Surely, she would want to be rid of us? But a lot of this was about keeping secrets. She didn't want anyone to know how she was treating us. The lady from Social Services was nice, and sure enough, she asked who we wanted to live with. My brother did as he was told and answered that he wanted to remain where he was. For some reason, I didn't do what I was told and I answered that I wanted to live with my mother.

I don't know if my stepmother did anything as a result of that, but my father did. I remember him taking me on his lap in our kitchen. This was exciting for me as he never usually did anything like that. As I snuggled into him, he told me how disappointed he was that I didn't want to live with him anymore and how he didn't love me because I'd done that. This was the first time I'd been explicitly told I was not loved. In fairness, I'd already reached that conclusion anyway so it shouldn't have come as a surprise. The problem was, my father had never done anything to me. He'd always been fine. In many ways this made it mean a lot more because it was him saying it.

Now I had explicit evidence that my actions led to someone feeling bad. Up until that point it had been implicit; I had learned through observation.

Sometime later, my brother and I went to stay with my mother for the summer holidays. At the end of the holiday she asked if we'd like to stay on and live with them. This seemed too good to be true, and we both said yes enthusiastically, not believing it was actually going to happen. Apparently, the point at which I told the Social Services lady that I wanted to live with my mother, I was classed as legally old enough to make that choice. Because I spoke up, we got to live with my mother and her husband. In no time at all we were asked if we wanted to call this man 'dad'. We didn't, but we daren't say anything. Now we gained a stepfather and a mother. He was a long-distance lorry driver and was rarely home.

This was an oasis in the landscape of my childhood. For around a year I was fed well, played out with friends, loved school, and didn't live under the threat of violence for everything I did. Do you remember the plot twist thing? Well, it's time for another one.

We're all screwed up (and that's ok)

My stepfather lost his job. As a result, and for reasons I am unsure of even now, we moved back to North Wales. If that year was the oasis, the return to Wales signified returning to the deepest desert. With all that extra time at home it was clear that my stepfather was emotionally abusive, and, because of our past experiences, this carried with it a very real threat of violence as a consequence.

My mother is disabled. She was born with a bit of her spine missing, and while we were living with my father and stepmother, she had a series of botched operations. This left her in constant pain. She also had Colitis meaning she could have really bad reactions to certain foods. This meant that she was limited in what she could do around the house. We were soon given a whole series of daily chores. Chores had to be done exactly to my stepfather's high standards, otherwise he would lose his temper and we'd have to repeat the chore. I had to iron his shirts and any crease in them, or the collars not being done exactly right, resulted in many more hours over the ironing board. We had to make his packed lunches for work. They had to be buttered right to the edge and very specific combinations of fillings had to be on them. Because we had experienced very physical consequences in the early part of our childhood, we were very obedient children for my stepfather. I firmly believed, by that stage, that my behaviour could make things worse, or better. I believed that I had control over the way my stepfather felt. I believed it was my responsibility, and therefore my fault, if I got into trouble.

We can now increase the count to four adults that either abused me, or were indifferent to abuse. Let's keep going.

When I was around ten years old my stepfather came to wish me goodnight. Only this time it was different. When he went to kiss me, he forced his tongue into my mouth. From that night he said he was going to teach me what boys did to girls. Every night he did more and more. I would switch the light off so I could hide in my head. I never had to do anything to him, and he never went as far as raping me, but he did everything else.

Like any abuse, and like the neglect and violence from my stepmother, this was shrouded in secrets. I always fought and resisted, even though it never worked. He began to use the chores as punishment for my lack of cooperation. One day, with my mother's approval, he took a belt to me. The pretext was that I wasn't doing my chores well enough, but when he took me into my room, shut the door, and pulled my pants down, he made it very clear that this was a result of resisting too much at night.

I was shocked. How could my mother let this happen? After everything we had been through.

When the abuse had been going on for a couple of years, I told my mother what was happening. She lost her temper with me. As I begged her to get me out of there, she responded with anger. She told me that we should never speak about this again. I sat on my bed after that conversation, feeling utterly helpless. I also felt that nothing I knew was right. Maybe what he was doing was not a bad thing? Maybe it was me. I learned that I could not trust my own feelings. If I felt what had happened was wrong, and my mother told me to pretend it never happened, then I must be wrong. By now, not only had I learned that I was responsible for others, I had learned I couldn't trust myself. You can imagine how this can lead to a lifetime of "people-pleasing", where you are treading on eggshells around everyone, and too scared to be yourself. I believed that I could really mess people up by saying or doing the wrong thing. I really thought I was that powerful. It's ridiculous really. However, as I have said, it's something that is so fundamental and so well-reinforced, that I still struggle with it now.

From the age of twelve to sixteen I have no memories at all. I took what she said so literally that my brain shut down. I recently reconnected with an old school friend from those days and had to ask her what to call her. I couldn't even remember that.

So now we are up to five adults. Five adults. Not a single one of them protected me, or put me first. Five chances for someone to care for me. Five times where they didn't.

Whilst my brother didn't experience the sexual abuse from my stepfather, the rest was enough to tip him over the edge and he ran away from home when he was sixteen. He lived on the streets for many years and has been a drug addict and alcoholic ever since. That is how he escaped. I was left at home, all the responsibility on my shoulders. When my mother was particularly scared of my stepfather, she would come and hide in my room.

I took a different path to escape. I went to University and got out that way. My brother and I both dealt with our demons in different

113

ways. I tried drinking and drugs, but nothing actually helped me escape my head, luckily!

As I grew up, I didn't directly feel unlovable. I just hated myself. I felt worthless. I felt I was too useless to even kill myself. I didn't worry what others thought about me. I knew they couldn't see how rotten I was inside. What did worry me was the effect I might have on other people if I let them get close enough to be 'tainted' by me. I kept myself distant and avoided sharing my inner thoughts for fear others would realise how rotten I was inside.

I went to University, and then had a hugely successful career. I was outgoing, confident and capable. That was externally. Internally I was nothing but a ball of pain and hatred.

Then I had my daughter. From the first moment I loved her unconditionally, as I know only a parent can. As she grew up and her personality developed, I looked at her and knew I would do anything to make sure she wasn't hurt. I would take anything on myself. I would unreservedly protect her, physically and emotionally. I looked at myself in the mirror. How rotten, and evil, must I have been that I didn't inspire a single adult in my childhood to feel that way about me? Because it wasn't just one person, I couldn't write this off as a screwed up adults doing screwed up things. People saying it wasn't about me didn't register. I get that for one person, but five? How could that be about anything other than me?

It has taken me a long time to let go of that belief. For everything everyone said, I had a counter. How can any adult fail to have that protective instinct around a child? Let alone five separate and uniquely motivated individuals. In the end, it was a simple concept, and help from a fellow therapist that helped me break through that belief. As I grew up, I had become two very separate people. Adult me was happy. Thanks to Cognitive Hypnotherapy I had let go of most of the demons. I was happy. I loved my family and friends and they loved me. Life was really good. I wasn't experiencing trauma flashbacks. I wasn't on high alert. I was calm, confident and happy. And yet, if anyone said anything nice or complementary to me, I dismissed it. They were commenting on what they saw. They couldn't see the rotten child inside of me. If someone dared to suggest I deserved happiness or success, I reacted with anger. How dare they! It seemed so unfair for them to say something that was so blatantly untrue. It was cruel and it hurt.

I realised this had to change. So much else had changed, this was holding me back. Since I had my daughter, I have been very clear that it is one thing me being screwed up, but I would not allow that to screw her up. At the time of writing this book she's ten years old, nearly eleven. By the time I was ten years old, all the worst stuff had happened or was happening. I regard it as a huge achievement that she is happy and balanced and nothing bad has happened to her.

In response to a discussion on a forum with my fellow therapists, where I raised this issue, I drew the rotten monster that was inside of me. She was six years old. I looked at that drawing. I hated her. I hated everything she represented. Then my friend and I were talking late one night on Facebook Messenger, and she handed that little girl a teddy bear. I suddenly found myself in floods of tears. No one had ever been kind to this little girl before, especially not me. The little girl clung tightly to the teddy bear. Over the next few weeks, I worked with my friend to help the little girl. We kept involving other parts. The twelve-year-old and the eighteen-year-old all came into play. For the first time in my life, I did not feel I had a rotten core any more. The different parts of me had started to combine into the real me. As I accepted the little girl, I stopped feeling broken. I stopped feeling rotten. And, lastly, and most importantly, I stopped feeling that I was the sort of child that nobody could love. Ana Forrest, the founder of Forrest Yoga, went on her own healing journey that had some similarities to my work with my younger self. She did a vision quest and, as a result, she killed off her inner child, in quite a brutal fashion. I understand that it was right for her, yet even now, with everything I know, I find the idea of killing the younger version of yourself quite impossible to accept. All our parts are just doing the best they can. They need the love and unconditional positive regard that you might often have been lacking.

Anyway, changing my impression of this child away from rotten to happy and carefree, and, most importantly, safe, created a fundamental shift in who I was from day to day. For example, there had been an underlying anxiety that I felt whenever I thought of speaking up for myself. When I went to meet with my daughter's school, my stomach would be in knots and I would physically shake. When I was at University studying for my Masters in Psychology, if I thought about asking a question or answering a question, once more my stomach would knot up and I would physically shake. Because of this, I rarely spoke up. This may seem hard to believe as I am more than happy doing talks to large audiences. I've even done a TED talk. The catch was, I assumed that all the content I produced would be ignored, or disagreed with, by most people. If people commented on my Facebook page, I assumed they would be disagreeing with me. This all changed once I no longer had a rotten monster inside of me. I have a new calmness. For the first time I stood up in front of a room full of people and talked about my past calmly. It was no longer me admitting to everyone how horrible I was.

At the end of the day, my childhood just sucked. I was super unlucky. This is the lesson that I help my clients to learn: events may have sucked, it doesn't mean you did. There is a huge difference between circumstances, and identity. I think that sometimes, the incongruence between how you think you should be feeling, and how you actually feel, can cause more of a problem than the feeling itself. For example, the other day my daughter came home in tears because she hadn't won a poetry competition at school. She was sure she was better than the kid she went up against. I told her that it totally sucked that she hadn't won, but I was really impressed by how hard she had worked on learning it, and how good she was at reciting it.

I could have told her that she shouldn't be upset. I could have diminished the significance of the competition to try and make her feel better about it. However, that wasn't going to help her much in the future with other stuff she did. She was already trying to say she never won anything. She's ten. Of course, she hasn't won much. Black and white thinking is the first sign that the subconscious is involved: I NEVER win ANYTHING". Instead I told her it was okay to be upset. I would be upset too. It didn't mean she'd done anything wrong or could have done it any better. It just meant that circumstances didn't work out in her favour this time.

This is such a difficult concept to take on board because the only person in your head is you, so naturally you are incredibly self-centred. Everything you hear, see and do is put into the context of your own personal experience. For example, I might ask you what you think about the naughty step as a punishment for children. The naughty step is where you put a child on a spot and they are not allowed to move. Generally, you do it for as many minutes as their age. A five-year-old would be on it for five minutes etc. The intent is to give them time to calm down and reflect on their misdemeanour. Your attitude to this form of punishment will depend on your own personal experience growing up. You will validate your feelings with logical arguments. This is Cognitive Bias. Cognitive Bias, in simplest terms, is where you look at the world through a very specific filter of your own experiences. If I asked you to describe the taste of a strawberry, you would immediately conjure up an image of eating a strawberry. If you like strawberries, you would describe it as pleasant. If you don't like strawberries, you will describe it as unpleasant. There is no factual content in there as to whether a strawberry is nice or not. However, you will believe that what you say is factual and correct and will, no doubt, argue your case if challenged.

Cognitive Bias is often used in Social Media algorithms. On Facebook, the algorithm will look at things that you have interacted with positively through likes and shares, and show you more of them. It wants you to use Facebook as your main source of information. This means that although you believe you are receiving a spread of news and stories about a general topic, you are, in reality, only being shown the stuff that matches your unique bias. Google is the same. Google's success is based on it being the place to go for information. The whole search algorithm is based on providing accurate matches for your search. For example, if you were to search Donald Trump on Google or any Social Media platform, you are going to get one of three groups of results:

1. If you are a fan of Trump, then you will get matches related to positive things he has done.
2. If you are anti-Trump, then you will get matches related to negative things he has done.
3. If you have shown no particular interest in Trump in the past, then the searches are as likely to return a match to things from before he was president.

The problem with Cognitive Bias is that you rarely have any awareness that it is going on. We all tend to fully believe our own Cognitive Bias. This bias can lead you to believe the thoughts you have in your head. When the thoughts make you feel bad, you seek evidence of other examples to validate that feeling. This fuels the bad feeling in the same way as you fuel a fire. When you find yourself thinking "this always happens to me", or "Nothing ever works out", become aware of the bias in your thinking. Black and white thinking is the first clue.

Even though a common therapeutic approach is to work with the inner child, most of the time it's not relevant to work with the child as a whole. Sometimes we just need to work on a single, or a small chain of specific memories with a connected meaning. However sometimes, an entire period of life has too many memories to single them out, combining episodic memories, traumatic memories, and core beliefs into forming a solid identity. In these situations, it's about working with parts and helping the different parts to see things differently. This is not a cognitive process. Rationally and logically pointing out that other people are screwed up and that you can't control behaviour may be technically understood, but it's the hurt part that needs to hear it, not the thinking part.

As a result of priming, and cognitive bias, a lesson learned in childhood about being loved less because of an event, can quickly snowball into an identity level believe that you are unlovable. This belief then becomes a permanent filter to every experience you have in life, only allowing through those things that reinforce the belief.

This is most common in clients that have had an abusive childhood. In some cases, a parent has explicitly stated that the child was not loved, or not wanted. In other cases, the child has inferred it from a parent's behaviour.

I had a client whose mother had struggled with depression her whole life. This was such a debilitating illness that they often took to their bed for days. When functioning, they were so insecure that they would ask the client what he thought about their clothes, or their hair. Of course, there was no answer my client could give that didn't cause trouble. If they said something nice then the mother would keep on at them until they said something that was easier for them to believe. Eventually my client was forced to say something not so great to the mother, at which point she would fly off the handle and cry. As my client grew up, this made him feel responsible for his mother's happiness. He felt that if he could just say and do the right things, then his mother would love him more. Eventually the mother took her own life, sealing the fate of my client who had spent a lifetime desperately trying to make everyone happy and to make everyone like him.

The belief that it was anything to do with him was purely an illusion. Many clients with an abusive childhood become very good at watching the adults to try and not set them off. They believe if they say or do the right thing, then they won't get hit, or shouted at, or punished, or guilted into feeling bad. If it was really true that their behaviour affected by that of others, then they would get abused once and never again. After all, why on earth would someone continue to do behaviour that got them in trouble, if they had the power to stop it? It is therefore impossible to hold on to the belief that you are responsible for what people think about you, and that you would be crazy enough to use that responsibility in such a way that you end up suffering. You have to believe it was not something you could control. Nobody in their right mind, if they had control, would make that stuff happen. With this client, I guided him to help his younger self see that his mother loved him regardless of how she behaved and how he behaved. With an objective, outside guide, it was easy to find examples of things his mother did that reflected that she loved him. Knowing that he was loved meant that he couldn't hold on to the idea that his behaviour made him unlovable. Letting go of the belief that his behaviour was wrong or bad meant that he no longer took responsibility for the feelings of those around him. He could see that everyone had their screw ups and that it was nothing to do with him. It allowed him, for the first time in his life, to be okay with being himself.

Feeling unlovable is not always connected to a bad childhood. Whilst there is plenty of evidence to say a bad childhood leads to problems as adults, there is very little evidence looking at whether a good childhood leads to problems as adults. As many problems are caused by implicit meaning or expectation from childhood, as are caused by explicit abuse, both verbal and physical. It's not what happens to us, it's the wrong meaning taken from what happens that causes the problems. We need to look at expectations from wanting to please much loved parental figures, in the same was as we look at how neglect and verbal abuse set expectations, to establish where the belief in being unlovable comes from. Looking at it this way is similar to the approach used by Positive Psychology, where studies and practices focus on what makes you happy, rather than what makes you unhappy. Positive psychology is "the scientific study of what makes life most worth living". All too often in therapy, the focus can be on what is wrong, rather than what is right. This can mean that people avoid seeking help because they compare themselves to others who have had a difficult time, and assume they should be happy. I share my personal story so that people can see that no matter what has happened, it's still possible to be happy. Too often society believes that you will be permanently stuck with the consequence of your negative experiences. Once depressed, you'll always be depressed. Once you have anxiety, you will also have to battle it. Unfortunately, people sometimes say to me "I feel bad because I haven't had anything bad happen to me, unlike you". Each experience is unique to you. A friend betraying you can feel just as traumatic to you, as being beaten by my stepmother feels to me. The way you feel is based on your model of the world, and your experiences, not mine!

In 2016 Age UK published the results of a study that showed over half the population surveyed said they are reminded of their grandparents by retro refreshments and nostalgic nibbles. Food is a powerful emotional trigger. It is particularly effective for triggering positive episodic memories. Quite a few clients that come to me about weight loss have very positive childhood memories. They may have had a close relationship with their mother or their grandparents. Often the tangible signs of how loving those relationships were, are circumstantial. For example, when I am out, my daughter and her dad usually stay up late, eat chocolate and watch films together. Because her brain is not fully developed yet, it can't interpret this as a loving connection, and will lock on to the tangible aspects of it, such as eating chocolate. In the future, eating chocolate will remind her of her loving relationship with her dad. As grandparents can get away with things that parents would never do, it's very easy for fond memories and associations to be formed around food and love.

One of the areas that can cause children a significant problem related to love is when parents split up. As adults we understand how difficult and emotional the end of a relationship can be. If you have been through a split like this when you had children, the decisions become even more difficult. Often parents will try and stick it out for the sake of the kids, or try and keep the split hidden from the kids until the last possible moment, as they believe this is protecting them. Children are not daft. They can tell when their parents are not getting on. However, because of this need to make things about love, and because we are all innately selfish, the children will be reaching their own conclusions. It is quite common for a child to believe that their behaviour is the cause of the problems, especially where arguments will often centre around the kids. As a consequence, they may also then believe that if they say or do the right thing, they can keep their parents together. I have had many clients who have felt personally responsible for their parents splitting up.

What makes this even trickier is that you are human. When you are going through any sort of relationship break up you are mentally and emotionally in a bad place. Of course, you are. It really sucks! Whatever you believe, in this state you are not thinking or acting rationally. Children will not understand this. They will only understand that you are maybe a bit snappier with them, or you let them off with things they've never been able to get away with before because you're distracted. They will be learning from the situation whether you are speaking to them or not. If you don't explain, then they will take their own meaning from it, and it will be about them. This all comes from good intentions of trying to protect your children from the "adult" stuff. However, it is rarely taken that way. The kids don't have the experience you do.

I have had a number of clients that felt unlovable as a result of their parents splitting. The irony is that often they have had a great relationship with both parents after the split.

Dawn C. Walton

You are in a far better place to be a parent
when you aren't miserable all the time.
Unfortunately, the quality of the relationship
does not cancel out the meaning encoded in the
memories as they happen. One thing that adults
do, in an attempt to be fair, is give the child a
choice as to which parent becomes the primary
carer. This is an impossible position for a child,
that lacks adult understanding of consequences,
and is equating everything to how much they
are loved. It's a catch 22 situation. They
perceive that whichever parent they choose,
the other is going to feel that they love them
less. Can you imagine how it feels to go through
your whole life feeling you have betrayed the
person that looks after you, so much that they
no longer love you? The clients that I have seen
with a situation similar to this in their past, can
present with a range of debilitating issues
ranging from anxiety and depression, to Chronic
Fatigue Syndrome where they lack energy to
function and have to fight constant pain.
Helping them see that parents splitting has
nothing to do with how much the child is loved,
releases them from these states. It's a lot easier
to understand this as an adult too. In our
sessions, I get the adult version of them to help
the younger version see the situation in a
different way. This lets go of the meaning in the

memory, making it sit harmlessly amongst the millions of other autobiographical memories that are stored as they grow up.

In our house, I use the term "I love you even if..." in a liberal way. I am attempting to make it impossible for my daughter's subconscious to create a LOVE EQUALS BEHAVIOUR or LOVE DOES NOT EQUAL BEHAVIOUR relationship from any event in her life. I want to make it impossible for incorrect meaning to be attributed to anything that happens. Examples include: "I love you even if you have ketchup on your face", "I love you even if you say you hate me", "I love you even if you've done a smelly fart", "I love you even if I've just shouted at you". It doesn't matter how big or small the behaviour, or whether it belongs to me or her, she knows that nothing means anything about how much I love her. I love her no matter what.

There was a particularly amusing event when she was four years old. We were leaving her friend's house and she'd been having a great time and really didn't want to leave. If you are a parent you will be familiar with the level of tantrum possible when a child wants to carry on what they are doing. Usually we try and get them to calm down by promising them that they can come back another time. Of course, this doesn't work because a child's brain is not developed enough to understand a consequence like that: "hang on, you want me to stop having fun right now for the promise of having fun again at some future point in time that I don't even understand!". Unsurprisingly, the tantrum continues. On this occasion I think I'd bribed her back to the car with chocolate, which had created enough of a distraction to get her into the car, but not enough to change the fact she was upset about leaving.

She was in a child seat in the front of the car with me. She was writhing around and crying, and then suddenly grabbed the gear stick of the car. I drive an automatic so it didn't have much of an impact, but it could have. I pulled the car over and sternly told her that she had just done something that was never acceptable. I remained calm, recognising that she was in an emotional state. I just needed to be clear that she had crossed a line. Initially she was shocked, but then she reverted to her tantrum.

"You're 'hobbirle'" she cried. She had such a cute way of saying horrible.

"You're lovely", I replied.

"I hate you", she screamed.

"I love you", I replied.

You see, her opinion of me, or whatever she was saying in her emotional state, had nothing to do with what I thought of her. I love her no matter what. I continued to counter, calmly, with positive affirmations related to how I saw her. I repeated that I loved her no matter what. I explained that we were leaving whatever, so what she said or did would not change that. She soon calmed down and we were able to continue the journey home as if nothing had ever happened.

At the time of writing this book, my daughter is ten years old. She knows, without doubt that I love her no matter what. This gives her total security that no matter what she says, or does, it will not change that I love her. In fact, when she's around her friends and their parents joke about not loving the child because they've done something rude or naughty, she's shocked. She can't believe that someone would tell a person that they didn't love them because of something they did or said. I hope that when she's older, no matter what she struggles with, it will never equate to her being unlovable.

Dawn C. Walton

Time travel Superpower

The third superpower that people believe they have is the ability to time travel. I can guarantee that you believe you can time travel. How? Because I know that at some point, possibly quite often, you have said "I should have..." or "If only I had..." or "I wish I hadn't...". To review past events and decide that a different outcome might have been possible implies that, at some level, you believe it's possible to replay moments of your life.

I can tell you now, time travel is not possible. I know this because nobody has come from the future yet (really hoping that this is still true as you read this book else this whole chapter is going to read very differently!). Even if you could time travel, have you ever watched a time travel film or read a book with it in? You might have noticed that small, seemingly insignificant changes often lead to catastrophic changes further down the line. I often discuss the film Sliding Doors with my clients when we are talking about time travel. In the film, the lead character plays two different roles. The first role is of a lady who gets off a train at one stop. Half of the film is about that version of her. The other half of the film is about the same lady, but she gets off the train at a different stop.

That's the only difference, but the whole path of her life changes. The Butterfly Effect is another good film about time travel, where the main character attempts to change the course of his life by repeatedly changing different aspects of his past, but it never goes right.

You can really get yourself into a mess if you try and get your head around what time travel would really mean. You need to be honest with yourself though. For example, it is generally true that people with anxiety are predicting the worst possible outcome of a future situation. The anxiety comes from the belief that you might be able to do something to mitigate that outcome. In reality, you are so busy thinking about the next possible scenario that you are never present enough in the moment to deal with what is happening right now. Time travel is a kind of opposite of anxiety. You believe that if you could go back and re-do a moment in time, then everything would have worked out brilliantly, and there would have been no hurt or damage.

Really? Knowing what you know about time travel, how could you possibly believe that you could know the all the alternative outcomes from any moment in time. Yes, it could have been better, but equally it could have been way worse. Undoubtedly the one truth is that if anything was different in your past, you wouldn't be the person you are today. And which moment would you change? How can you know every single possible outcome from every single moment in your life? You can only know what did happen, rather than what could have happened. This has to mean that in every moment of your life, you did the only thing you could have done. To believe anything else would mean you had the benefit of hindsight or 'do-overs'.

It's not really your fault that you believe this. It's caused by the way the brain is wired. This comes back to the memory system of episodic and autobiographical memories. Try this for me: Don't think of a pink elephant. I bet you thought of a pink elephant. If not, you thought of a blue elephant or a different animal. There is no longer any version of you that has not done the task you just completed for me. Your brain has been permanently updated with that memory. Tonight, while you sleep, that will be processed, along with everything else that has happened in your day, and ordered into the huge database of your life to pick out things with meaning that you need to remember. You can't remember everything. Even the human brain isn't capable of that. You just need to remember the important stuff.

Everything your brain learns and stores overwrites what was there before. There is no revision history or ability to track changes like you have when you are working on a shared document with someone else. This means that every time you recall a memory you change it. You add to it what you now know. It can also be changed by what other people say when you are recounting a memory. This modification replaces the memory that was there before, leaving no trace of the original. Have you ever watched an audio file play on your phone or on the computer? There is the 00:00 start point, a line and a bunch of waves representing the sound, and then an end point, let's say 03:45. When you press play you can watch a line move towards the end point. You can see how much has played and how much is yet to go. If that audio player was the brain, the 00:00 point would move with the line. You would lose sight of how much had already played. As a result of this constant overwriting, you believe that the person you are today is the person you've always been. You believe that the way you reacted to things in the past is the same as the way you react today. You treat today as evidence of what tomorrow will be like. You use today to judge the earlier version of you.

Let me tell you a story of a time I ate an apple when I was around seven years old. I have already mentioned that food was sparse when I was younger. I remember that generally, when I ate an apple, I would eat everything except the stalk. I even ate the pips, although a part of me, at that age, was convinced a tree would grow in my tummy. Actually, I liked the idea of an apple tree growing in my tummy because it would mean I would have an endless supply of apples. Anyway, back to the story. On this particular day I was eating my apple when, a few bites in, I spotted half a worm hanging out of the apple. I remember thinking that it must mean that there was the other half in my mouth. I spat out what was in my mouth, and I ate around the space occupied by the remaining half.

Many years later, when I was an adult, someone offered me an apple from a bowl of fruit. I declined, saying that I didn't really like apples. They asked me how anyone could not like apples. This story popped up in my head and I told them what had happened. They immediately pulled a disgusted face. "Eww, I would have been sick" they said gagging. After that, whenever I thought of the apple and the worm story, I also thought of my friend's reaction to hearing the story. In fact, I'm not sure any more that I didn't actually gag a little. I'm not sure if I did carry on eating the apple or not. Maybe I never ate an apple after that day. The reaction of my friend, as I told them the story, had overwritten the memory that was there.

Every time you talk about something you change it in some way. You add your understanding, or another person's reflection on it. If the memory happens to be an episodic memory, then it is likely that you add to it in a way that gives it more significance. As the previous memory has now been overwritten, next time the episodic memory is triggered, it is even more significant and robust. I once saw a client with a really high level of anxiety in social situations. Their previous therapist had told them that the anxiety was about attention seeking. From that point onwards, whenever they felt anxious, they also felt terrible about themselves because they thought they were doing it on purpose for attention.

This re-writing of your memories is called reconsolidation theory. It is in action all the time, particularly when you talk and when you write. It's a little less significant when you just think through stuff because thoughts are so intangible, it's hard to separate truth from fiction.

This is why therapies based on just talking can be so hit and miss. When you first talk through something there can be a sense of release. Expressing something and bringing it out into the open can diminish the power it holds over you, compared to keeping it in your head. Then you have your next session and expect to feel the same level of diminishing release. However, now you just bring the same memory forward again. Instead of diminishing it, you add to it. You add your own understanding that you have gained since the last session. Maybe you have been reading or talked to friends. Maybe that thing you talked about has triggered a bunch of autobiographical memories and their associated episodic memories, meaning you remember more. You go into the session and bring forward the memory with this added understanding. Your therapist then offers their opinion, based on their experience and the way they see the world. Their words enhance and change your memories and you leave the room with them stored back in a different way. Of course, you don't realise that they are now different, because they are your memories after all. Each session you repeat this cycle, continually ensuring those memories are at the front of your mind. Continually changing them both deliberately and inadvertently. This can have dire consequences if you don't realise it's happening, as with my "attention seeking" client.

In 2005 my husband had reached a point where he was fed up with my level of misery. He told me I really needed to get help. He could see something in me that I'd never been able to see in myself and he was desperate for me to see the same. As a result of my childhood, there wasn't a single thing I liked about myself. I constantly thought about killing myself. In fact, the only reason I hadn't was because I knew I could. It was kind of comforting to know that there was always an option to escape if I needed it. I used to joke that I wish I would be run over by a bus, but always lived somewhere that wasn't on a bus route!

He found someone for me to see and, after I had spoken to her on the phone, I went up for my first session. She was a person-centred counsellor. This approach is based on empathy and unconditional positive regard. It doesn't use any techniques as such. For a year and a half I went to see her every two weeks or so. She listened and reflected on what I was saying.

She asked questions which I gave a lot of thought to in between sessions. For that period, I was constantly thinking about everything that had happened to me. Talking felt good. At various times in my childhood I had been told not to talk about stuff that was happening, so it felt like a huge release to be able to safely talk to someone. What I didn't realise was that she was adding to my memories as I spoke. Sometimes this was constructive and diminished them. More often it added extra dimensions to those memories.

Fifteen years after those sessions, I still remember one particular session. I was telling her about an incident that happened, as an example of the sort of abuse I had experienced. The incident happened in the bath, and as I painfully described it, believing it was important to tell her (and expecting her to react badly and kick me out of the session) I struggled to find the words. She decided she would help. She nodded and said "slippy". Fifteen years later I still remember that word, her face, the position of her body and the memory, as clearly as if it just happened. The memory itself has become more blurry over time, but that word keeps that part of it strong and clear.

If you were to ask her to remember 'that session with Dawn where you spoke about that thing', she would be unlikely to remember most of it. She definitely would not remember what she said. I doubt she wrote that in her notes after. But I remember it. My brain has been permanently updated. That memory has been permanently updated. Even as I write this down, I am aware of a change in my body's state. I am shaking. This is the power of reconsolidation theory.

Years later, now a qualified therapist helping hundreds of people every year, I get why that worked that way. I am very careful not to impose my opinions and views onto my client's memories. When we talk about things, we do so to intentionally diminish and change them.

Reconsolidation theory is not just applicable to talking, it also kicks in when writing things down. A common therapeutic tool is to journal. The theory of journaling is that by writing stuff down it can lose its power. It also gives you something to read back at a later point in time when you have experienced enough change to have lost sight of how things used to be. Like talking, writing gives thoughts substance. Re-reading what you have written down can change the way you see things. It also makes physical changes to the brain. If I say to you, "next time you go out don't notice any white cars", then you are now going to notice white cars. As an aside, I once told a client based in New York not to notice any yellow cars. Must have been feeling particularly cheeky that day!

In 2013 Amy Bleuel founded the semi-colon project. The semicolon was chosen because in literature a semicolon is used when an author chooses to not end a sentence. It was supposed to represent that people were choosing not to end their lives. People had semi-colon tattoos on their wrist, to show they were still fighting, despite what had happened in their past. The problem with these tattoos is that they are a constant reminder of what you have been through. Even if you are feeling great right now, a single glance at your wrist will trigger episodic memories connected to times where you have struggled. When I hear about the semi-colon project, it was obvious to me that it would just be creating an anchor to a bad memory. I couldn't understand why people were so enthusiastic about it. In 2017 Bleuel killed herself.

We get what we focus on, so whatever you write becomes a stronger focus. This is neuroplasticity: your brain is constantly, physically changing as you learn and forget. Neuroplasticity is what allows someone who has brain damage, such as a stroke, to fully regain all physical and mental functionality. When brain damage occurs, you do not repair the damaged part of the brain, but physically grow new neural pathways.

To understand how neuroplasticity is always in action consider the following example:

You like to walk your dogs every day, and your route takes you through a huge field. Every day you dutifully follow the path that runs right around the side of the field. The field is never used for anything, but that's where the path goes, so that's where you walk. One day, you don't have as much time as usual to walk the dogs, so you decide to cut right through the middle of the field. It's a bit hard going. The grass is overgrown and the ground is uneven, but it takes so much less time, you are happy that you did it. The next day, you decide that you have been daft to always take the outside path. You are going to cut through the middle of field again. It's a little easier this time because you've already done it before. The grass is flatter. It's easier to see where you are going. Other people notice this new path, and soon everyone is cutting through the middle of the field. Soon, the old path grows over, until eventually it is so overgrown you would never know it was there. The new path is well worn and everyone now uses it.

Every time you actively notice something you are travelling a path. This neural pathway becomes thicker the more you use it, making it easier to travel. When you don't use a neural pathway it gets thinner, until it eventually disappears. When you journal, you are more likely to travel the worn path, and notice those things that are the way they have always been. You may write down some new stuff, but you also write down the old stuff. If you reinforce both paths, the worn one remains the easier one to travel. This is the challenge with journaling. It can keep you in a pattern of travelling down the worn path.

A gratitude diary can also have benefits. With a gratitude diary you would be standing at the head of the field saying to yourself 'it's great that I have such a lovely field to walk the dogs in'. This makes you feel good, but it doesn't do anything to the paths. Gratitude is not evidence based and therefore does nothing to the wiring of your brain. What it might do is release serotonin, the happy drug. That is a good thing but is for a different discussion. For neuroplasticity you need to deliberately choose to reinforce the positive paths that you would prefer to travel. My advice, if you are journaling, is to only write down positive, evidence-based observations on your day, not an inventory of everything that has happened.

It is judgement of earlier memories, and earlier versions of you that can lead you to feeling bad about yourself. You can't see, because you can't time travel, that an earlier version of you did the only thing they could at that moment in time. Which brings us back to the problem with believing we can time travel. Because the brain is constantly, physically being updated, and because there is no record of what was stored there before, we tend to regard our memories of particular moments as absolute. Most people don't understand that every memory you have, and every interpretation you make of a situation, is totally subjective. It is based, not just on the age you were at the time, and your understanding at the time, but also the layers of understanding that you have added to it since. Each one of these layers overwrites what was previously there with new meaning and understanding. This happens outside of our conscious awareness, and is something that most people struggle to understand. In fact, sometimes a client may say to me "I am not sure if this really happened but...". I explain that nothing is true and nothing is false. It's not actually relevant whether the event really happened. The structure of episodic memories ensures that the meaning is locked in irrespective of the facts around the event. As it is the meaning that causes the subconscious to switch off the brain, then the facts are largely irrelevant, until you want to change the meaning.

A belief that we can time travel stops us learning from events in our life. Instead of learning that you survived, or that you could handle failure, or whatever, you end up focussing on what you should have done. An even more debilitating scenario is where you spend your whole life beating yourself up for doing something, or not doing something. This means that you totally miss any achievements or skills you have in the present.

There are two significant areas where the time travel belief can cause enough of a problem to limit your life choices. These are depression, and fear of failure/procrastination.

I am not a big fan of labels. Labels can be great in the early days of diagnosis. They give you a sense of belonging and normalcy; 'I am not the only one with this'. They can also provide validation for how you are feeling (and they give you something more concrete to Google!). However, labels are not solutions. They are merely a categorisation of facts into one, convenient term. If I discover one day, that I have a cut on my finger, then I can say I have a cut, or a wound or an injury. It doesn't tell me how it happened, and it doesn't tell me what to do about it, but at least I can say, "I have a cut on my finger".

If I go to the doctor and tell them that I seem to have lost motivation to do anything, I struggle to get out of bed, and I don't see anything good in my future, they are likely to tell me I'm depressed. From now on, I don't need to tell people I have lost motivation, can't get out of bed and have no hope, I just need to tell them I'm depressed. I also filter everything that happens through my new label: "This is because I'm depressed", "I can't do that because I'm depressed". In time, the only version of me that I know is the depressed version. I may, occasionally think back to the days when I wasn't depressed, but it will get harder and harder to remember what that was truly like. So much so, that I can't see a future where I am anything other than depressed.

As with the cut finger, I don't know why I'm depressed, and I don't know what to do about it. I just can clearly define what this current state is, and know that other people have experienced something similar, hence the use of a label.

The doctor will probably prescribe anti-depressants. These are tablets that adjust the chemical balance of your brain to prevent you from feeling chemically too low. If you are a woman, you will know that once a month your hormones go a bit out of whack. This can mean you get a little (or a lot) grumpier and more emotional. Just for a few days. There have been situations where this hormone imbalance is so extreme that a woman has ended up being sectioned, because they are a danger to themselves or others. They are literally not in their right mind. Despite this, I have countless friends that every month say "I don't know what is wrong with me, I have such a short fuse" or words to that effect. We just assume that we are rational and in control most of the time. Without the hormone balance being off, you get back to 'normal' and are able to think your way through stuff again. Then you realise that the reason for your mood being of was just a regular temporary thing. Despite this, the next month, the same thing happens. This is very similar to what happens when you are depressed. The chemical balance is off and that makes it harder for you to cope with things. With this balance out of whack, it can make it nearly impossible to work on why you feel that way.

Tablets are the equivalent of putting a plaster on the cut on my finger. The plaster covers the wound meaning nothing can get into it and make it worse. This is really important if the wound is too open. The plaster does nothing to heal the wound. It merely stops it getting worse. This is the same for anti-depressants. They do nothing to address the root cause of the depression or to accelerate healing. They just stop it getting worse.

For this reason, in the UK, once someone is put on anti-depressants, they often remain on them for the rest of their life. They may be offered, and go through, talking therapy counselling. In the UK, this is usually Cognitive Behavioural Therapy. This therapy approach focuses on behaviours and how you can think your way around them and out of them. With this approach, just under half of the people improve enough to be signed off from counselling within 6 months. Given that they have often waited over a year to begin the treatment and given that only a very small percentage of people experiencing depression will seek help, then most people with depression are not given any solution to get out of it. Once labelled with depression, it is often a label you keep for life.

There is a reason for becoming depressed. In this reason, lies the solution to breaking the cycle. It comes from a belief that things could or should be different. 'Should' and 'Could' are words that imply time travel. They imply that something might have played out differently. Depression comes from this comparison. It is either a belief that you **should** be coping better, versus what you believe the reality is. Or it is a belief that you **should** be somewhere in life, compared to what you believe you have achieved so far. It is the expectation that causes the problem, not the reality. This is why when everyone tries to make you feel better by pointing out all the things that are good in your life right now, and all the good qualities you have, you don't hear them. In fact, it just makes you feel worse, because they are talking about reality and you are thinking about your expectation. All they are doing is making the gap between reality and your expectations of yourself appear wider.

This expectation comes from somewhere. It comes from lessons you have learned as you were growing up. It comes from comparing the way you see things with an episodic memory that has some meaning, related to not being good enough. If you don't change the expectation, then the problem with reality will continue. If you don't work out what you did to cut yourself, then you risk continually cutting yourself. A plaster will protect the cut, but it won't stop you cutting yourself again, and it won't make cuts heal quicker. In the same way, tablets will stop the chemicals getting so low that you stop being able to function at all. They won't do anything to address the reason you are depressed in the first place.

Depression comes from a mis-match between expectation and reality. Expectation is a problem because it implies you could have done something in different way. It implies time travel.

I am not the sort of person that is motivated by other people's achievements. I look at people in a similar field that are more successful than me and think "It's not fair. I can do that as well as them, why am I not successful?". When I worked for a large corporation, I would often come out of meetings wondering how people were in senior positions when they were clearly incompetent. Instead of being inspired to beat them, I would feel it was pointless to even try. After all, I'm not the sort of person that things work out for. Nothing ever goes right for me.

This black and white thinking is often the first indication of a problem that comes from time travel. It can be challenged by the phrase "Is that really true?":

Is it really true that NOTHING works out for me?

Is it really true that EVERYONE is more successful than me?

Is it really true that I am NEVER going to be successful?

What would others say if I asked them? Would they see it the same way as me? Of course not. I know for a fact that there are others that are in awe of what I have achieved. Every time they say something about how amazing I am, I do a comedy-style double take in my head, "Me? Don't you realise how useless I am?".

We don't see things as they are. We see them filtered through the meaning that comes from our own model of the world. This model of the world is constructed from our timeline of experiences to a small degree, but to a greater degree is caused by the meaning in our memories. It is caused by episodic memories.

I have, stored in my brain, a unique perception of who I am and how I come across. I compare that to how others come across. I don't notice the good things I do. There is no value in that from a survival point of view. I am only looking at those things that might make me feel rubbish about myself. I weigh them up and either take corrective action to sort out my perceived problem, or sit and stew in my head, grumbling at the world. I would love to be the person that can feel happy for the success of others. But I'm not that person...yet. I have a narrative that runs in my head based on my experiences. I go back to my childhood experiences. These are experiences where I didn't matter. These are experiences where nobody cared enough about me to fight for me. These are experiences where I was not listened to, and not believed, in relation to some really significant stuff.

As a result, I learnt not to speak out for myself. What is the point? No one will listen anyway. It doesn't change that I want to be heard. It doesn't mean I don't have anything valid to say. It just means I assume that I know how people will respond, so I don't even try.

This isn't true. There is little evidence for these thoughts in the present. However, I am weighing things up through my own unique filters. If the evidence I see does not match my experiences and my expectations of myself, then I discount it.

We all do. Maybe you've been worried about how you look, and someone close to you says you look fine. You ignore it. Maybe you've been to a performance review at work and you've been told an area you need to improve on. You probably walked out of the meeting feeling a bit rubbish about yourself. You probably didn't think of all the positive things you were told. Your mind takes you straight to the negatives.

This is what happens with depression. The mind is so busy looking at the past and where you should be, that you fail to see the present and where you are. It is the word "should" that is the problem. If you can change the way you remember the past, then when the brain searches for a match to the current situation, it no longer finds one. Without a match, without an alert point, you maintain the ability to be logical and rational. This stops your brain being switched off and prevents the emotional response. The gap between expectation and reality becomes smaller and eventually disappears, allowing you to accept things that happen in the present moment. In the last chapter, I will provide some exercises that you can work through to change episodic memories.

The other issue often caused by a belief we can time travel is a fear of failure. A fear of failure can show itself in a number of different ways, although it essentially comes from a similar root in your memories. It is based on a belief that you are not good enough.

My brother is nearly two years older than me. He went off the rails quite significantly from aged fourteen onwards. This was his response to our childhood experiences. When he was sixteen and preparing to take the first significant exams in his life, my mother and stepfather recognised that he was capable, but had no interest in his exams. They decided to incentivise him by offering him money for each exam he passed. They said he would get £10 for each exam he passed, and £20 for each exam he got an A in. In the end, he ran away from home before he sat his exams. A couple of years later, it was my turn to take my exams. I was studious and quiet. I didn't cause any fuss. As a result, I was not offered any incentive to do well in my exams. When I got three A's, five B's and a C, I got nothing to say well done. It was just expected.

This was obviously incredibly unfair. It is also an episodic memory as it is a memory that has a lot of meaning attached to it. It could have sent me into an over-achieving frenzy, in a desperate attempt to prove myself as worthy as my brother, or as important. Equally I could have decided that no matter how hard I try, no one notices, so why bother? I could have stopped making an effort and began failing so that I would get the same level of attention my brother had received. After all, if all behaviour serves a purpose, then even negative behaviours have a place if they get you attention. However, in comparison to all the other stuff I was dealing with, this was nothing and I didn't develop any compensatory behaviours as a result of that moment in my life. I do, however, remember it very clearly and feel very wronged by it.

A sense of unfairness in a childhood event has been the basis of the problems for many of the clients I have helped. If you are accused of something that you didn't do, what lesson can your subconscious learn to protect you from getting in trouble again? Normally you work on cause and effect: when x then y e.g. when you hit a kid in class, you get sent to the head. If you didn't do x but y still happened, then that is an impossible situation. If you didn't hit the kid, but still got sent to see the head and got in trouble, now what? Eventually you learn that nothing you do is right and anything could get you in trouble. When you get in trouble for doing something that someone else started, this can lead to a feeling of helplessness, and a sense of injustice that can be very intense, depending on the circumstances. This is further complicated by the lack of development in your pre-frontal cortex.

It is fairly common for a child to be accused of doing something they didn't do, especially when they have siblings. There is a natural jostling for position, competing for the attention of the parents or caregivers. My brother was great at crying as soon as he was accused of anything. I never cried. When we got in trouble and my parents were trying to find out which one of us to blame, I always looked like the guilty one. My brother would cry and blame me. I would deny it but with no emotion.

It is also fairly common in school where you are surrounded by multiple comparison opportunities in the form of your classmates. If someone does something in a class of 20+

children, the teacher has to decide how to approach it. They will have a natural bias against some kids, and natural favouritism towards others. If that teacher has a bias against you, or if one of the other kids has mastered the art of lying convincingly, then there is every likelihood that at some stage you will get in trouble for doing something you didn't do.

I know this is a normal part of growing up. Because of the job I do, I have a different level of understanding around the problems it might cause in later life. When my daughter first came home from school upset, because she had been told off for something she didn't do, I explained that teachers are human. Nobody knows a true story unless they are actually there, and even then, they will see it in their own way. This is why you have multiple witnesses in a trial. Also, to the teacher, it's not significant to incorrectly accuse a child of something they didn't do. It's not even a big deal to the child, unless they are already carrying an idea that there is something wrong with them and they will always be the one that gets blamed for everything. Note that when dealing with unfairness, or indeed many other problems, the first clue around irrational thoughts is, once more, black and white language: "everyone hates me", "I always get in trouble", "No one ever believes me". This wide sweeping generalisation is part of priming, where you only see what you are looking for. With my daughter, the first thing I do is call her out.

Daughter: "Everyone hates me"

Me: "Really? Everyone? I don't hate you"

Daughter: "Ok, well everyone at school hates me"

Me: "Really? Everyone at school. Does the teacher hate you?"

Daughter: "Ok well all the kids hate me"

Me: "Every single kid in the school? Even the ones in the other class that don't know you?"

Daughter (getting frustrated): "No. Obviously not. Just all the kids in my class"

I then work through the names of all the kids in her class, including the ones I know are her friends, until we get down to one name. In this example, one kid in the class hated her. And that was a kid that she didn't like and didn't want to hang out with.

It's a normal protective response, when feeling that you are not good enough, to back off and protect yourself from being hurt. The first stage in finding out why that behaviour is coming through, is awareness.

When my daughter was upset because she'd been accused of something she didn't do, I gave her a strategy for the future. I pointed out that there were, I was sure, many things that she had done that she'd never been found out for. All she had to do was mentally swap out one of the things she had done, but not been caught for, with this thing that she was being unfairly accused of. It would be a fair swap and would lose the sense of unfairness. Since that conversation, I have never heard her say something was unfair, or demonstrate any sort of behaviour around that. In fact, in many ways, she has gone too far the other way where she is fairly indifferent to getting in trouble, even when she has actually done something!

A faulty perception of the meaning of success or failure often drives behaviours at work or when studying. If you believe nothing you do will be right, no matter how hard you try, then you are only left with a couple of options.

Firstly, you can give up trying. What's the point in trying if it's only going to end up in failure anyway? It can be hard to understand how procrastination and laziness could serve any sort of positive intent in the subconscious. Consider, for a moment, I tell you that you have won millions on the lottery, and that tomorrow morning, bright and early, you need to take your ticket to a particular office and go and pick up your winnings. I would be very surprised if you procrastinated about that. You would clear every obstacle to ensure you were there. This is the thing about procrastination or only putting a half-hearted effort in, it only tends to be applied to things where you can equate the result to your efforts to yourself and your abilities. It affects the way you see yourself.

This is a common problem in weight loss clients. I once had a client that had done countless diet programmes. Every time they lost four stone or more, they started putting it all back on again. When we talked, it became clear that they identified themselves as the 'fat friend' in the group. Losing four stone meant that when they looked in the mirror, they looked slim. They lost an identity that they had carried since school. As we don't like uncertainty, it was more comfortable to put the weight back on and know their place in the social group. All behaviour serves a purpose. The weight helped them maintain their identity.

Often the reason for keeping weight on, and the excuse it provides for not exercising, or socialising, or taking care of yourself, is way stronger than the vulnerability you might feel for being in control and solely responsible for your own success or failure. You don't have many friends because you are too fat. That's easier to believe than you don't have many friends because not many people like you. You can't join that exercise group because you are too fat. That's easier to believe than accepting that you are too unhealthy to keep up with the class. You can't go for that job because nobody would take a fat person seriously. That's easier to believe than admitting you have not got the skills or capabilities to get that job.

Sometimes the fear of success is as strong as the fear of failure. It leaves you nowhere to hide. You have no excuses. I had a client that had struggled with their weight their whole life. They had, on many occasions, lost significant amounts of weight. Then, as soon as the effect of the weight loss was visible, they would put it all back on again, and some. We did our work together to clear the emotional and self-esteem aspect of their weight issue, and once more, as soon as they started losing a significant amount of weight, they began to switch to different behaviour. The difference this time is that I was there. This client was in a bad relationship. If they lost enough weight, they would have no reason to stay. They could leave, build a new life, meet a new man. Their weight gave them an excuse to avoid rocking the boat. After all, who would be interested in them while they carried all that weight? We sorted that aspect out, and the client continued to lose the weight, left their husband and moved away to build a new, happier life.

It's a lot easier to accept that you failed because you didn't put enough effort in, than because you weren't capable enough. Technically, you could put more effort in, but there is nothing you can do to address not being good enough.

I had a client that had struggled with a lack of confidence and self-belief. It was a challenge for him because he looked around at the other people he had worked with and felt frustrated that he knew so much more than them, and was so much more capable than them. Yet here he was, too scared to go for a promotion, and too scared to change career to something that he was more passionate about, because he did not believe he was capable enough. Like a drop of food colouring in a glass of water, the belief spread. It went beyond work and into his relationships. As he talked, he talked about "nothing" ever working out for him. He talked about the inevitability of "always" being alone. He looked at his friends that were "all" in happy relationships, and there he was, having just split up from his girlfriend, destined to be alone "forever".

If this belief in not being good enough was absolutely true, then he wouldn't have been sitting in my therapy room. He would not feel sad or depressed. The problem was caused by a part of him that knew that wasn't true. This other part wanted something better for him. It aspired to him being a better and happier version of himself. It was the conflict between these parts that was causing the problem, not a certain way of thinking. This is where the awareness comes in.

We asked where is the hurt coming from? Why is a part of him so focussed on him not being good enough? If all behaviour serves a purpose and all behaviour has a positive intent, then what possible intent could be served by him feeling so rubbish about himself? I have previously mentioned that the subconscious is both primitive and well meaning, but learns lessons about what will hurt you as you are growing up. It was clear that at some point in his childhood he had been made to feel not good enough. This would hurt because we all feel okay until someone makes us believe we are not! In an underdeveloped mind, you lack the ability to cognitively understand context, circumstances, personal bias, emotional bias etc. You are learning important lessons that you will carry with you for the rest of your life, when you are not capable of understanding the lessons you are learning. To say this is a bit of a problem is an understatement!

With this client I knew that it was not true that he would never have a good relationship. It was not true that all his friends where happy and settled. It was not true that everyone was more successful than him at work. In fact, he was very successful. He worked for a company where he managed a large team of people, and had done for a number of years. But he wasn't able to see any of that. His subconscious was priming him to only notice what was wrong about his life, not what was right. This was a protective response to stop him being hurt further. If we were to release him from this limiting belief, we first needed to get to the root of where it came from.

When talking about his earliest memory that related to the feeling of not being good enough, we went back to an eight-year-old version of him, standing in the classroom. He was trying to read out a passage of text from a book. He was normally really good at reading, and was not feeling nervous or worried at that moment in time. However, on this occasion, when he tried to read out the paragraph his words became all jumbled up. The teacher then started to tell him off for messing about. They criticised him in front of everyone else, for not working hard enough and doing enough preparation. Eight-year-old him was mortified. He felt embarrassed and worried about all the other kids thinking he was an idiot.

In that moment in time his subconscious learnt a lesson. It learnt that it sucks to feel that you are not as good as everyone else. It must be true, because it was a teacher, an adult, who was saying it. Feeling rubbish was not the real problem here, however. There are lots of things that happen as you grow up that make you feel sad, or angry or frustrated. The real problem was that he didn't mess up reading the paragraph intentionally. He had actually been trying his best to read it out properly. If you have tried your best at something, and you have been criticised or made to feel rubbish for that, then where do you go from there? How do you correct that so that it doesn't happen in the future? This is where a belief in time travel comes in. It is not uncommon for a well-meaning adult to say something like "I know you are capable of so much more" or "if you just put enough effort in then you are capable of anything". I say well meaning, as these phrases or pep talks are designed to inspire and motivate. However, they imply the ability to have performed differently than you actually did. They imply time travel is possible. If you have tried you best, and your best is not good enough, then your only option is to be left believing that you are not good enough. This is what had happened with this client.

My client believed that no matter what he did it wouldn't be good enough. This led to his subconscious trying to keep him away from situations that might make him feel like a failure. But that was only a part of him. The other part of him knew he could do this stuff and really wanted to. He was in a constant battle with himself. And the problem with that is that the protective part will always win in a battle with a positive part.

If we could get the protective part to realise that he was good enough, if he could let go of the belief that he "should" have tried harder or studied more, then we could get rid of the hurt. Without the hurt there is no need for protection. Because of neuroplasticity and "don't think of a pink elephant", it's very easy to change the way you remember things. Because we can't time travel, we can't change what actually happened, but that's not what is causing the problem here. The problem comes from the incorrect meaning in that memory, not what actually happened. If we can change the meaning, we can change the impact it has on his day to day life.

As the adult version of him reflected on that memory, with my guidance, we could see that it was wrong of the teacher to have a go at him for such a random and insignificant thing as reading a passage of text. Everyone messes up sometimes. That's normal. Making a big deal out of it is not normal. Why should the adult version of him be limited by something a random teacher said that had no meaning and no significance? I am 100% sure that if you tracked down that teacher and asked them "Hey do you remember that day you told that kid off for messing up reading out that paragraph?", that they would have no idea what you were talking about. Why would they? It had no significance to them. This means that there is no value in him continuing to store this memory in this way. The brain only learns and attaches meaning to stuff that hurts.

To change the memory, we need to remove or change the emotion. If you have ever read Harry Potter, you will have read about the way to deal with the Boggart. A Boggart is a magical creature that changes it's form to match your greatest fear. In the books and film, when Remus Lupin, who is a werewolf, looks at the Boggart, it turns into a moon. He then casts the Riddikulus spell to make it into something that holds no fear. In the story it turns into a balloon that then flies away. With my clients we need to do the equivalent of the Riddikulus spell. With this teacher, we needed to make her sound as ridiculous as the thing she was saying. The simplest way to do this is to change the way you remember the voice. Common choices include Donald Duck (have you ever noticed that when Donald gets angry, his feathers go red. How is that possible?), like they've breathed in a helium balloon, a Minion from the Despicable Me films, or even to slow the voice right down and make it very deep. I should imagine, as you read you might be thinking of something someone said that hurt you. I should imagine also, that without consciously trying, you have now changed that voice into something silly. This will fundamentally change how that memory is stored. In this case my client changed the teacher to sound like a Minion. The thing I love about the Minions is that they are impossible to understand, as they speak their own language. Changing the voice in this way not only made his teacher sound silly, she also became impossible to understand.

Once you have changed the way you remember something, you change the meaning. It is impossible for the same meaning to hold true when the memory did not happen in the same way. Meaning is also cumulative. In this moment my client learnt he was not good enough. From that point onwards, every similar moment validated that lesson as being true. This meant that by the time he was old enough to leave school and be responsible for himself, he had a rock-solid catalogue of evidence to support the theory that he was not good enough. He also had something very robust for his subconscious to keep him away from. He was primed to only notice that he wasn't good enough. Any successes were ignored and discounted as irrelevant, or excused away with a "yeah, but...". When you change that first, earliest memory, then all structures built on it will also collapse, in time. Next time he was ignored, or messed up, his brain will try and access the early memory to decide how to respond. It will find nothing of any significance, and will allow the cognitive part of his brain to remain engaged. Even before he left the session, this client was beginning to see some of his achievements, and his perceptions of his friends and the relationships he'd had were beginning to change too.

Another possible response to feeling like you are not good enough is to go out to prove everyone wrong. When you take this path, you become an overachiever at everything, striving for perfection in whatever you decide to turn your hand to. Unfortunately, those who choose over-achievement are looking for external validation of their success. That is something they can never find because it doesn't come from the right people or in the right format. Those who strive for perfection feel just as much a failure as those who avoid effort, as their expectation will never match the reality

People often assume that problems as debilitating as depression and low self-worth must come from a terrible experience growing up. This is not necessarily true. I have seen many clients where their parents were so loving and nurturing that they were left with a terrible fear of letting them down. Internally they constantly measured everything they did against a check of "Will my parent be proud of me?". Men tend to be more prone to feeling like a failure, especially if they had a strong and respected father figure growing up. The problem is the bar is set too high in their brain. It is an implicit bar. The parent never explicitly stated their expectations. However, as you grow up, you learn more by example and by the meaning you extract from events, than by what is explicitly stated. I don't think there are many parents that are trying to make a child feel terrible when they bring them up. It is far too easy, unfortunately, to inadvertently make a child feel you are disappointed in them. This is particularly easy to do around exam times.

I know, as a mother, I believe in my daughter. Her ability to think her way round a problem is more impressive than anyone I have ever met. As such, I know that no matter what she's struggling with, she will be able to find a solution. However, she's a kid and she's awkward. She hates homework and will do almost anything to avoid it. No matter how many times I tell her something, she won't listen. She's capable of anything she puts her mind to, but she's not capable of putting her mind to many things. Because I believe in her so much, it would be very easy for me to communicate that to her. I could tell her to just focus and work harder, because she's capable of more than she's delivering. The reality is that she isn't. She can only do what she does, nothing more, nothing less. My absolute faith in her could easily become the basis for her lack of faith in herself. What I try and do is express my belief in her, without any time travel implication: "I know you will work it out" or "you will do the best you can, no matter what happens".

I have worked with a number of kids around exams and exam nerves. One girl had an easy time at school. Despite being nagged by her mum to spend more time studying, she aced the first set of exams she took, without having to study. This made her feel like she was clever. Two years later, she was taking the next set of exams. She hadn't realised how much harder these next ones were. She ignored her mother again, and barely studied. When she took the mock exams, to check how ready she was, she failed all of them. She was devastated. She felt everything she had believed about herself, and how clever she was, was wrong. Her mother told her that she was capable, if she would just have studied. She didn't believe her mother. And she couldn't time travel to prove her right or wrong. If she'd failed her first exams, there wouldn't have been a problem. She would have learned what she needed to do next time.

Failure is an important part of the learning process. If you try and avoid failure, then the only thing you are failing at is learning. A young child can only learn to find their balance when walking, by falling over. In 1968 3M's Spencer Silver was working on developing an ultra-strong adhesive for use in aircraft construction. Instead, a mistake led to the new type of glue with a unique structure that allowed it to stick and be removed repeatedly. At most levels Silver failed, but as a result we ended up with post-it notes. Learning that you are not good enough prevents you from learning from your failures, as you are working so hard to avoid them.

At the end of the day, a belief in the ability to time travel stops you seeing what is really happening in the present. It also stops you seeing a positive future. If you can just accept that no matter what you did, and what happened in your life, you were the best version of you, then it will be a lot easier to let go of things.

Addictions, Trauma and self-harm

Up until now we have looked at the 'normal' screw ups that can get in the way of life. We have looked at this both from the structure of the brain and the organisation of episodic and autobiographical memories, and from the superpowers that we believe we have as adults that allow us to control our environment. Sometimes the cumulative effect of childhood experiences can be so significant that every moment of adult life can be a struggle. Sometimes, something so significant happens, that it can't be changed just by looking at it differently. Some things can't be explained away, they just suck. The pain of these kind of events in childhood can be so intense that it is almost impossible to live with yourself.

In this chapter I will look deeper into some of these things and try and help you understand what goes on in the brain when they happen. If you have had some bad experiences, this chapter may be a bit trigger-y so you may want to skip it if you don't feel in a good enough place.

Addiction

Imagine that there is a button on the wall in your kitchen. This is an amazing, magical button. Whenever you press that button you will change into whatever positive state that you need to be in. It's a great button because it can both create a feeling, and allow you to escape from a feeling. If you are anxious, the button will calm you down. If you are struggling with the thoughts in your head, your mind will go blank. If you are lacking in confidence, you will lose your inhibitions. If you are feeling sad and lonely, you'll feel uplifted and happy. With an amazing button like that on the wall, you would be crazy not to press it when you needed to. After the button has been there for a while, you learn not to worry as much about whatever state you go into. After all, you can just press the button.

The problem with the button is that there is a price attached to it. Of course, there is. All powerful magic comes at a cost. But the cost is something you pay later, not right now. And the problem you are facing is happening now. It's more likely that you will deal with your problem now, and worry about the consequences later.

We are driven by instant gratification. The subconscious is the instinctive part of the brain.

Instincts lead to instant responses. When faced with anything that hurts you, you instinctively do whatever is necessary to escape the hurt. It doesn't matter that there is a price to pay. You need to do what works now. Any addictive behaviour is the equivalent of having that magic button in your head. When you are hurting, or threatened with hurt, you will always press the magic button.

With some substances, the chemical released from the magic button is so powerful, that it creates a secondary addiction. This physical addiction means that even when there isn't a risk of being hurt, or any emotional need to press the button, there is a strong physical need and physical draw. This means that not pressing the button has physical consequences. If you struggle to cope at the best of times, then coping with this physical withdrawal will require additional support. Additional support that you would usually get from the magic button. And so, a physical addiction cycle is created.

Whilst it may feel this way sometimes, this physical addiction cycle is not an issue for most casual addictions. What I mean by a casual addiction is behaviour such as eating, drinking a couple of glasses of wine at night, smoking, and some drugs, like cannabis. For example, the nicotine in cigarettes, that is responsible for the physical addiction of smoking, is out of your system within seventy-two hours. Three days after your last cigarette you do not have a physical need to smoke. Most smokers who attempt to give up last longer than three days. Most can manage at least a couple of weeks before they smoke again. This means that that the thing that draws them back to smoking is not a physical need. It's a mental need. This mental need is set up, for most people, when they first turned to smoking as a teenager. The most common reason for starting to smoke, that I have observed in clients, is to fit in. Years later, when that need no longer applies, it's that memory of connection and belonging, or even rebelling, that triggers the lighting of a cigarette.

This idea that things are mentally addictive seems hard for people to grasp. You see high levels of judgement for people who smoke, are overweight and drink. "Just stop", people say. They tell you to eat less, or healthier, and move more; like you are stupid and have not even thought about that. They don't realise that you have a magic button and you need to press it. There have been many attempts to make smoking unappealing in the UK. Stark warnings and graphic images were put on the front of cigarette packets explicitly stating "Smoke this and you will die". That didn't change anything. The price of a pack went up massively. That didn't change anything. The first thing that had an impact on smokers was not being able to smoke in any public place. If you started smoking to fit in, then a change that means you are ostracised when smoking, means you are not gaining anything from the act of smoking. Pressing the magic button doesn't work so well. But you've always done it. This means that, whilst it is less effective when you do it, you still can't easily break the programming that makes you want to. You still want to press the button even if the button doesn't work very well.

One of the things that many smokers worry about is putting on weight when they stop smoking. There is a myth that smoking makes you want to eat less. If smoking was an appetite suppressant, the tobacco companies would be all over it. In the days where they were still allowed to advertise, you would have seen adverts along the lines of "smoke more, lose weight". Smoking is not an appetite suppressant. Smoking serves a purpose. It creates a feeling. When a person stops smoking, they don't suddenly and magically gain the ability to have that feeling. They still need to serve the purpose. They turn to a different sort of behaviour that meets the same purpose, often eating.

Not all addictions relate to substances that are consumed. Some addictions are purely behavioural. In these cases, there is no physical cycle to keep the addictive behaviour. Pressing the magic button does not, in itself, lead to a need to press the magic button again. An example of a behavioural addiction is gambling. There is no substance consumed and no physical component to an addiction to gambling. As online gambling has grown, gambling addictions have grown too. It is something that is now possible to do without anyone else knowing. You don't have to go down to the betting shop. A couple of clicks on the computer is all it takes. I have found this secrecy is very important for the clients I have helped with gambling addictions. If there is no physical component at all to gambling, why then is it so hard to stop? The answer lies in the purpose. If all behaviour serves a purpose, what is the purpose of gambling? Do you remember competing with anyone on anything? You probably had times, particularly when you were younger than ten, where you found yourself in competition with other kids of your age. This may have been a very clear competition: maybe writing a short story, or reading out poetry, or something else. Or it may have been implicit competition. Maybe you wanted to do better than the kid in the class that always seemed to be good at everything. Or maybe you had a nemesis that you felt beat you at everything. This need to be as good as someone else can lead to a lesson about yourself and not being good enough. This lesson can lead to a lifetime of measuring yourself against others, and striving to do better. It can also lead to a real buzz when you succeed. Recreating this buzz is the thing that is often underlying an addiction to gambling. This is the magic button. It's a unique buzz.

In this instance, in order to remove the effect of the gambling, so that it no longer serves a purpose, you need to remove the buzz. You need to make it so that hitting the button doesn't actually work. This is easier than you might think. Feelings come from inside of us, not from anything external to us. Imagine there was someone that you fancied. You see them most days, and over time you have built up an image of who they are, and how they would be with you that just increases your attraction to them. It is not based on anything other than your own perceptions, and not limited by anything other than your imagination. Every time you think of them your heart flutters, as your body chemically and biologically responds to the images flying through your mind. Your imaginary relationship with them becomes stronger and more intense over time. One day, you bump into them. Their breath absolute reeks. It's one of the vilest things you have ever smelled. They don't even try and apologise for bumping into you either. Now, the reality of this person intrudes on your imaginary world, destroying this idealised view you had. Soon you can't believe that you ever found them attractive, and you barely glance at them anymore.

Behavioural addictions can be changed this easily, as they are just based on the perception that something gave you a feeling. Perceptions are based on what you know at the time, and are very easily changed with additional information. When the perception changes, so does the feeling.

Some addictions are addressing problems you have via a direct physical solution, rather than a mental and physical approach. Alcohol addiction is an example of this. Alcohol addiction is on a spectrum that ranges from alcoholism at the most extreme end, down to the odd glass of wine that you have most nights after work. The key thing that makes anything on the spectrum an addiction is purpose. What purpose is the behaviour serving? At the most severe end, alcohol can be used to dampen, or even block out, painful feelings and thoughts. This is also true of some hard drugs such as heroin. It's hard to escape from your head. It's there with you wherever you go! You can't stop thinking and feeling. Closing your eyes just makes it worse. You either need to create a feeling that is intense enough to distract from the internal pain, or you need to kill off the thoughts and feelings that you are struggling with. Alcohol is good for dampening feelings and thoughts to the point of escapism. In this case, the magic button helps you escape from what is going on in your head. This can be true of drinking, hard drugs and binge eating; it is the mindlessness that is appealing, not the buzz or feeling that is created. With a strong physical addiction component this can become a cycle that is very difficult to escape from.

In my younger years I was desperate to escape from my thoughts. The pain was so intense sometimes that it was almost physical. Luckily, I had no access to anything that would help. I also believed that I had an addictive personality, and if I started on something, I would never be able to stop. I now know that there isn't really such a thing as an addictive personality. There is just a need to escape and a recognition that some things will help you do it. My brother, after he ran away, lived on the streets of London. To survive in that situation, you need to be less present. He started on the hard drugs and is still on them thirty years later, although now he is on the heroin substitute, methadone. Even when I did try drugs and alcohol, nothing seemed to be strong enough to get me out of my head. I'm grateful for that. If it had worked, I would probably not be here writing this book now.

If you want to overcome an addiction, you are likely to be less effective if you focus on the behaviour of pressing the button. Traditional therapies focus on this. Sit on your hands so you don't press the button. Walk around the room instead of pressing the button. Take a deep breath. Read a book. Go for a run. These are all cognitive functions that require choice. They are a bit like the anger scales used with children at school. When you are feeling mad walk away. This is great thinking, as long as you have your thinking brain still engaged. However, we have already established that when faced with any level of emotional hurt, the first thing that happens is that your cognitive functions are disengaged. This means that whatever coping strategies you have that focus on choice are immediately unavailable to you. This is why people who stop smoking start eating. It's just substituting one coping strategy for another. At the end of the day, life gets in the way. In those times where things get to too much, and your cognitive function is diminished, you will always default to what works; your addictive behaviours.

Too make it worse, once you have gone through the analysis of your behaviours and alternative, healthier coping strategies with your therapist, or from your self-help resources, you have a double whammy. You can now feel bad about continuing your addictive behaviour and feel bad about not executing on strategies to avoid your addictive behaviour!

If you want to permanently overcome an addiction, you first need to identify what purpose it is meeting. Instead of coping strategies around the magic button, you want to change things so you don't think about pressing the button, or if you do, it doesn't work. You need to get rid of the purpose of the behaviour.

The most common purpose served by many casual addictive behaviours is to de-stress. Stress is very subjective. What stresses me will be very different from what stresses you. What causes me stress has also changed very significantly over time. Many years ago, if I needed to find something in a department store, I would never ask a member of staff. Even the thought of going up to a stranger and asking them something would have me physically shaking. People have been scary most of my adult life, thanks to my childhood experiences. My best friend could not understand it at all. For her, walking up to someone and talking to them did not require any effort or thought. She would regularly stomp off in frustration to do the thing that I was incapable of. It caused so much anxiety for me that I would make sure I avoided situations like that if I could. I couldn't at work, but I had become very good at ignoring my limiting beliefs in that situation. I also found that once I had my daughter, I could do things for her that I would never do for myself. For example, if there was something missing from her food in McDonalds, I would go back to the counter and ask them to correct it. I would never had been able to do that if it was just for me. I referred to it as my 'front door complex'. I attempted to make every situation as familiar as possible, as I couldn't cope with not knowing how it worked. For example, if I was going somewhere new, I would do a recce the day before to work out where the entrance was.

This became really tricky when I was flying all over the world with my job, but it did come out in other ways, where I would be really early to meetings, and to airports and train stations. I also wouldn't use the toilet in a new office for the first day, and often I wouldn't eat anything if I wasn't sure what the eating arrangements were. By the time I'd been there a couple of days, I was able to follow other people as they went to the toilet (in a non-creepy way obviously!). I also never left the hotel I was in if I was on my own. I wouldn't eat in the restaurant on my own. And I wouldn't phone for room service because I wasn't sure about tipping the person who delivered it. I missed out on lots of experiences in some amazing countries because of these insecurities. I didn't take any substances. I just avoided situations, to the best of my ability, that made me extra anxious.

As I began my therapy journey, all of these things changed. I remember the first time I sat on a tube on the London Underground and did not have to tense up my whole body because someone was seated next to me. I remember being in meetings in work, and not freezing when someone casually put a hand on my arm. Of all the things, I think the most noticeable change came the day I'd flown into Belfast airport. I'd been there a couple of times before so I had a fair idea how it all worked. I usually took an aisle seat and didn't check bags in, so I could get off the plane, straight through and out. On this particular day I got off the plane and sauntered down the walkway towards arrivals. I looked out of the window and noticed what a lovely day it was. I saw an Ikea out of the window that I'd never noticed before. I was on my way to Enniskillen and needed to pick up a hire car. Once I was through arrivals, I realised that I didn't have the reference paperwork for the car hire company. This was most unusual for me. I would normally have everything printed out and checked. Even more unusual was my indifference to this realisation. I just shrugged to myself and figured I'd ask at each desk until I found the one where I was on the system. As it happened, it was the first desk I went to. I think part of me remembered which was the right company. Having successfully picked up my car and a satnav device, I then realised I had no idea where I was going. I had a hotel name and that was all. Once more I shrugged and decided it was such a lovely evening, I would just enjoy the drive.

The amazing thing about all of this was that it wasn't a direct result of a therapy session. I think it had been a number of months since I'd done any work. It was just part of the natural process of feeling more secure in myself. My stress triggers had disappeared. If I had been using substances to cope, then I would have found myself turning to them less and less, as the need to cope went away.

Stress is subjective. Think about what makes you stressed. Do you have a partner? Do they get stressed by the same things as you? I bet they don't. If you want to change an addictive behaviour, you first need to understand the circumstances that lead you to do it.

With smoking, most people start because they want to fit in, or they want to rebel. Forty years later, you have a family and circle of friends, but are stuck with the behaviour, because your subconscious is constantly taking you back to that moment in time as a teenager, where you felt you didn't belong.

With casual drinking, people often have a few glasses of wine to wind down at the end of the day. Does wine actually help you relax? Recent studies suggest that a glass of red wine every night can help you relax and sleep. Being calm, being relaxed, and getting a good night's sleep, are all important to help you with a healthy mind. But what if you could get all of those things without alcohol? Surely that would be better. Also, it rarely ends up as just one glass. All behaviour serves a purpose, so look into your life and ask what causes you to feel stressed in the first place. Changing your level of stress removes the need for the wine, meaning that maybe you could choose something like a brisk walk, or an activity with friends as a healthy alternative, that still delivers the mental health benefits. Also, removing a high level of stress does not just improve you mentally. Reducing adrenaline has a knock-on effect to improved blood pressure, and improved immune response.

With gambling it is usually about creating a buzz. Not everyone is into the idea of adrenaline fuelled activities such as rock climbing and jumping off bridges on bungee ropes. Adrenaline is released with anxiety, fear and also exercise. The key to overcoming a gambling addiction is to realise that the buzz that you get is generated internally and doesn't need any external artificial stimulant. I have dealt with a number of clients with a gambling addiction. They are predominantly male. I'm not sure if that means that it's one of things that it's okay for a man to admit they have a problem with, or if it is something that more men experience. In all instances, the client has been trying to recreate a feeling that they had when they were a child. For example, one was trying to recreate the buzz of their football team winning, and tended to predominately gamble on football matches. Another was trying to recreate the sense of achievement they had over their mates when they won on a slot machine in an arcade when they were a teenager. That client predominantly gambled online. In all cases, focusing on the feeling rather than the activity was key to helping them overcome the addiction.

Eating is often not regarded as an addictive behaviour. After all, it's the only addictive behaviour that you can't get over by totally abstaining from it! People who have no challenges with what, and how much, they eat judge those that do quite harshly. Just eat less and do more. It's that simple. But it's not. If addictive behaviour is serving a purpose, then food becomes much more than just fuel to those have an emotional relationship with it. It is just as much a magic button on the wall as drugs or alcohol. Food is also often used as an antidote to feeling stressed. The emotional connection it has can take you back to times of feeling loved, safe, or looked after. It can also be an act of rebellion. If food was restricted and you stole food or ate sneakily, then as an adult you might find that you reward yourself with food. As with gambling, they key to breaking this connection is to revisit the point at which a connection was made between love and a feeling, and recognise that food had nothing to do with that feeling. Feelings come from inside and your experiences. An inanimate object such as food simply cannot be key to a feeling. For example, if you remembered your grandmother giving you extra helpings when you stayed with her, then as an adult, when feeling lonely, you might consume large amounts of food, because having more reminds you of your grandmother. But it was never about the food, and far more about the love your grandmother showed you. That love was there irrespective of whether there was food or not. In fact, in many ways, making a memory such as that about food belittles the real meaning.

As long as you remember that all behaviour serves a purpose, and all behaviour has a positive intent, then getting to the root of an addiction is relatively simple. If you can remove the need to cope, then the magic button will sit their gathering dust. It is worth noting, however, that if you find yourself at a point in your life where you are really struggling to cope with something, you will always default to whatever addictive behaviour has helped in the past. You will press the magic button any time you need to.

Trauma

The more damaging addiction is one that generally interrupts the normal course of life. This type of addiction relates to silencing intense thoughts and feelings. The level of intense emotional pain that leads to escapism-based addiction does not come from an unhappy feeling. It comes from traumatic events, either in childhood or in adult life. A traumatic event, in my model of the world, is any moment in time where something happens that is so difficult to reconcile emotionally and cognitively, that your only option is to switch off. They are tipping points where you experience feelings that are so incongruent with what you are being told to feel, or expected to feel, that you can't reconcile and learn from them. My mother's reaction to learning about the abuse was traumatic for me. I spoke about something that was wrong, and that I didn't want to happen, and my mother got angry at me and told me that I shouldn't talk about it again. I could not reconcile what I felt about the abuse, with my mother's reaction to it. That's why my subconscious shut my brain down and cut off the memories from that point. It would have been impossible for me to accept that the

194

abuse continued despite speaking out about it. So, my brain sorted the problem by locking that knowledge away from me.

It is the meaning in these moments that makes them traumatic, not the technicalities of what has actually happened. If you were to describe a violent or horrific event to five people, what they might describe as the most horrific part would probably not be the same as the part that your brain translated into trauma. Direct and obvious violence are incredibly disturbing, but generally not as likely to alter the brain in the same way as when the violence is coupled with an emotional component. This is why most therapists that work with trauma do not start helping people until around six months after the traumatic event. The mind and body can work through the physical effects of a traumatic event very effectively. In his book, "In an unspoken voice", Peter Levine describes the process of shaking that allows the body to physically release the energy earthquake caused by a traumatic event. He cautions against intervening in that process because it can result in the energy being stored instead of released. It is a bad idea to try and contain energy. Like fast moving water, if you try and contain it, or block it, it will eventually burst through in a violent, uncontrolled way. Levine uses this knowledge in his therapeutic approach to safely allow his clients to process and experience the trauma in their body.

When you experience a traumatic moment, it is stored in such a way that it overrides all other, previously learned, episodic memories. All memories are not created equal. As you go through your childhood, you learn key lessons from episodic memories. The first time a memory with meaning occurs, the lesson is encoded. After that, anything that is similar builds on that first lesson, refining and reinforcing it. Eventually you have a very robust lesson, backed up by many similar situations. This gives your subconscious the best chance of ensuring you are well protected, even if the event you are now experiencing isn't exactly the same as the one where you learned the lesson. It's a form of algorithmic learning. This is the same as is used in Artificial Intelligence to allow a computer to go beyond the limitations of data, and turn it into useable knowledge.

You will have many different lessons stored by the time you are an adult. Your subconscious will then search your database of memories as you experience different things, to see if anything comes up that it needs to take action on. This means multiple lessons can coexist, only being called into play if the circumstances provide a match. For example, you may have a memory of eating cake at your grandmother's house. At the time, it felt like the cake was a sign of how much your grandmother loved you. You gained a link between food and feeling loved that is activated whenever you are feeling alone. You may also have a memory from primary school where your teacher asked you a question in class that you couldn't answer. They belittled you in front of the class. This led to a lesson about feeling humiliated in front of other people. As an adult, whenever you have to stand up and talk, that feeling of humiliation comes to mind and your subconscious steps in to try and get you away from that environment. Both memories are triggered in different circumstances and so can co-exist with no problems.

Most who have experienced sexual abuse as a child will have at least one traumatic tipping point. One night, while I was being sexually abused, my mother walked into the room. She asked what was going on. The light was off, because I always switched it off when he came in, and my stepfather was bent over me. I don't remember what answer was given, but I do know that she left the room again and closed the door, leaving the abuse to continue. This memory is as clear in my mind as if it happened yesterday, and yet it happened when I was eleven years old. The thing that makes this a traumatic memory is not the fact that I was being abused at the time. It's that I didn't want that to be happening, and I thought it was wrong, but my mother leaving the room with no action must mean that the way I was feeling was wrong. Otherwise surely, she would have done something? When you try and make sense of something, but don't have the capacity, you go around in circles until you have no other choice but to bury it. Over the first eighteen years of my life, despite a continued litany of physical, emotional and sexual abuse, there were only a few that became tipping point, traumatic, moments such as that one. I worked on them with my therapist and we changed the space they occupied, changing the memory forever. As a result, I can talk about them now with no emotion. It is like I am telling a story of something that happened to someone else. Not in a negative, disassociated way, but in a way where there is no meaning and they have no power over me.

These tipping points can also happen with violence. There is very little childhood abuse that does not contain emotional abuse at its core. While violence is awful, there is little to learn from something that is being done to you. It is purely circumstantial. It's the meaning the violence that is loaded with that causes the problem, and the trauma. For example, being told that you are clumsy while being hit and punished for breaking something, gives the beating far more significance than just being hit.

This difficulty in reconciling what you should feel, versus what you are feeling, is the reason that so many women experience trauma around the birth of a child. It is expected that a woman knows what to do when giving birth. It is expected that you will experience pain and exhaustion. It is expected that you will bond with your new baby, feed them, and love them unconditionally from the moment they arrive. When your experience does not meet these expectations, there can be an incongruence that can be very difficult to make sense of. The reality is that a hospital birth has you at your most vulnerable, in pain, with a room full of strangers making decisions, over which you have very little control, and very little capacity to engage in. As a result of a traumatic experience during birth, a woman can find it hard to connect with their newborn. That baby is the reason they have just been through hell. Once more, expectations from everyone around you is that you have worked so hard for the baby, that you'll be grateful that they are there. Expectations versus reality is so often the basis for the struggles we have, as we saw when we looked at depression. I have helped quite a few clients overcome their birth trauma, although they rarely come to see me for that. The problem with trauma is that there is no expiry date. Once trauma has been registered in the brain, it affects everything that comes after. When your child is ten years old, you don't expect to still be dealing with the knock-on effect of their birth. Unfortunately, unless the trauma is cleared, it is likely that you will be experiencing the effect of it for the rest of your life.

One of the worst things about childhood trauma is the longer-term physiological impact. In the late 80's Vincent Felitti, head of the Kaiser permanente's department of medicine in San Diego, and Robert Anda from the Centre for Disease Control and Prevention (CDC) both reached a critical conclusion at a similar time. They discovered that the physical issues their patients presented with, and the recovery rates from those issues, was not sufficiently explained by diet, medicine and exercise. The men were dealing with obesity, heart disease, diabetes and asthma amongst other ailments. Felitte began to conduct interviews with those who had dropped out of the programme for obesity and discovered that a majority of 286 people interviewed had experienced sexual abuse. It seemed that eating was more a coping mechanism for depression and anxiety because of life experiences, which is why a simple change of diet and increased exercise was not enough to create change.

Felitti and Anda then went on to increase their sample, surveying over 17,000 volunteers about their childhood experiences, and matching to their health records. For the survey, they came up with ten categories of childhood trauma, that they referred to as Adverse Childhood Experiences, or ACEs. These were: physical abuse, sexual abuse, emotional abuse, physical neglect, exposure to domestic violence, emotional neglect, household substance abuse, household mental illness, parental separation or divorce, incarcerated household member. From their study they found that those with four or more ACEs were associated with addictions such as smoking, alcohol and drug abuse. There was also a correlation with health issues such as depression, heart disease, stroke, diabetes and an overall shortened life span. As a result, they concluded that it there was way more merit in attempting to mitigate the impact of these traumatic events during childhood, than investing in research for new medicines.

The problem with childhood trauma is the high level of stress it creates. We have already established that the stress response is designed as a short-term solution to an immediate threat. As such, it fundamentally alters your physiology to give you the best chance of surviving an encounter that may harm you. These physiological changes are not designed to be sustained on a long-term basis. Your blood is pumped around your body at speed so that you have the necessary energy to fight or run. Your pain response is altered so you do not have to stop for wounds. Your immune system is pumped up so that you can fight infection, taking the focus away from viruses and other diseases that may need something more long term. As an adult, whilst this response often goes on a lot longer than designed, it does at least reset to default when the stress diminishes.

When the same stress response is activated in a child, it can become permanently part of your physiology. You have not had the chance to establish a default resting state for your body. You are still at the learning stage. This means the bar gets set higher on the cells. The cells are physically encoded with a permanent alert state, so even when the stressful situation has passed, the stress levels remain high. The default is set to highly stressed. Felitti and Anda refer to this as 'toxic' stress. It is this toxic stress that can lead to health problems in adults.

The idea behind the Adverse Childhood Experiences movements is to raise awareness of the impact of trauma during childhood and, through ensuring those who work with children are trauma informed, mitigate the impact of the traumatic events on the child. By helping the child cope, when they are out of the stressful situation they can return to a more natural default, and avoid the physical implications of their experiences.

Trauma can also happen as a result of a random, unlucky event. I watched a video on Facebook the other day that was a story of a local drunk. This guy lived in a village in Russia. He was known as a homeless drunk. He slept in entranceways to blocks of flats to escape the cold. Most saw him as a pest and kicked him out at every opportunity. All except for one guy. When this guy came across the drunk passed out in front of his door, he invited him in and gave him a cup of tea. He talked to him and learnt a bit about him. It turned out that the homeless guy was quite a good artist. Curious, his rescuer spent time learning all about the man that no one wanted around. He told the story of a really bad car accident where he had been driving and his wife had died. He couldn't cope with the idea that he had killed his wife, and so began drinking. Soon he had lost everything and was in a permanently drunken state. His rescuer found out that he had a daughter, and he tracked her down on Facebook and reunited them. The drunk man is no longer a drunk and now lives with his daughter, who was very happy to find her dad again after years without him. All behaviour serves a purpose.

Trauma changes the brain. This change is reversible, but until then it can have a profound effect on all aspects of your life. Most people who have experienced trauma, also experience flashbacks. These unbidden, intensely emotional memories can stop you in your tracks, very much taking you out of the present. It is a common side effect for soldiers with PTSD, where a noise, smell or even an accent can take them straight back to that moment. This can sometimes lead to a severe panic attack, which is also known as an abreaction.

I learnt early on to disassociate from my body. I learnt that having my breathing restricted was a bad thing. I learnt that there was a darkness in my thoughts and if I remained still for too long, the darkness overtook me. When I was at University, I was hanging out with the man who would later become my husband. I can't remember the circumstances, but he had suggested I lie on the floor and he would talk and relax me using hypnotic language. As I lay on the floor, I started crying. This was not the reaction my husband was hoping for! I don't know why I was crying. I wasn't aware of any particular emotion. I just know it just sort of happened. That was the first moment that I realised that relaxing and having my eyes close might have a very different meaning to me.

The next time I stepped closer to that darkness was with the Person-Centred Counsellor that I visited regularly for about eighteen months. One day, quite far into my therapy journey with her, she asked me something and I felt everything shut down. A darkness engulfed me. I could hear her talking to me, but I could neither move to acknowledge her, nor respond verbally. It was terrifying. It seemed scary for her too as she kept calling out my name, looking for a response. I gradually emerged, first gaining the ability to open my eyes, and then move my head and look at her. She had other clients waiting, so as soon as I was able to respond, I had to get up and leave the room. I had no idea what had happened. I now know that this is how I do an abreaction and it's what happens when I start talking or thinking about something that is close to the space held by the traumatic memories. As I drove off from the session I was wondering where the nearest cliff was that I could drive off. It was an awful state to be in and I didn't go anywhere near it until a few years later when I was training as a Cognitive Hypnotherapist. I was working through my personal transformation, supported by Trevor my therapist. I was at a friend's house, who was also a therapist, and it was well into the early hours of the morning. We were talking about various things and I was expressing my frustration at not being able to close my eyes and engage in the exercises during the training. Whenever we learnt something, we practiced with a partner. Whilst I could apply the stuff I learned to my partner with no problems, whenever she tried to practice on me, all my defences went up. I wouldn't even close my eyes. My friend pointed out that, maybe, closing my eyes had a different association to me than to other people. Then suddenly I was in an abreaction again. Whenever my stepfather came into my room to 'say goodnight' I would switch off the light and close my eyes. I would hide in my head. When I had that abreaction, my friend was brilliant. She sat down next to me and gently talked to me, being in tune enough not to use physical contact and make things worse. As she talked, the shutdown worked its way through my body from stillness, to shaking, to being able to move my eyes and eventually talk. I knew then that no matter how bad that state was, I could get myself out of it.

I took that to Trevor, and we dealt with the abreaction in a therapy session, one that was truly awful, but necessary! I thought that was the end of my abreactions, until a year or so later, after I had mostly completed my cognitive hypnotherapy training. I was at a course on how to use cognitive hypnotherapy for childbirth. One of the main tools was self-hypnosis. This involved closing your eyes, doing some counting, and taking yourself into a relaxed, happy place. The more you practiced, the easier it would become. As the instructor talked us through this, I realised that there was no way I was going to close my eyes. 'That's fine', I thought, 'I'll just do the exercise with my eyes open'. However, as with that very first time with my husband, I found tears forming as she spoke. I could not do the exercise. I just thought about something else. It was incredibly frustrating.

I now know myself well enough to warn people what is happening if I am triggered into one of these responses, and I know I will get out of it. I know that it is likely to be triggered if I am trying to verbalise something my subconscious thinks I shouldn't talk about. It is a protective response designed to help me avoid an intolerable level of emotional pain. In 2006 when I first had that reaction, I didn't know any of that, and it was really scary.

Over the years I have become very aware that not everyone can move into a relaxed state easily. People have different associations with being relaxed. I have also learned that trying to reframe episodic memories, when there is a history of trauma, results in changes that seem to work, but don't "stick". When I have a client that should experience widescale change from our sessions, but still finds themselves triggered, I now look for a traumatic memory, or tipping point, where something was too emotional to deal with. We need to clear that before the changes we have made to the episodic memories will have a permanent effect.

The problem is, traumatic events can't be reframed. For example, if you change the voice of a teacher that made you feel stupid, to a ridiculous voice that you can't possibly take seriously, then you can't feel stupid. Someone with a silly voice is not going to teach you there is something wrong with you. No meaning means that it just becomes a regular autobiographical memory rather than an episodic memory. This is referred to as reframing the memory. Traumatic events contain so much emotion, or they are just so bad, that there is no way you can see them any differently. You are hijacked the moment you even try. These memories cannot be made to be ridiculous or insignificant because, in most cases, a client would not even be able to 'look' at the memory. This is back to the algorithms that the mind uses. It is not physically possible to remember everything that ever happens. It is not even physically possible to remember everything about a traumatic event. There will be a tipping point which turns a memory from 'this happened' to 'this means that…'.

Traumatic memories are so significant, that they cannot share a space with other memories. Have you ever played the card game Top Trumps? In this game you have a pack of cards that all relate to a certain theme. These themes might be cars, or superheroes or something else that has multiple dimensions to it. The way to win the game is to always put down a card with the highest or best number, because that allows you to steal the other person's card. The winner of the game is the one with all the cards. For example, if we were playing top trumps with food cards, maybe our cards include potatoes, chocolate, broccoli, and cheese. I have the card with potatoes on it in my hand. I need to pick something about potatoes that I am sure will beat other food groups. The data on the cards contains the normal attributes that you find when you buy food from a supermarket: sugar, fat, carbohydrates, calories. If I was to pick sugar, chocolate would beat it. If I pick calories, broccoli will beat it. I pick carbohydrates because I know potatoes are very high in carbohydrate. Now, whichever card my opponent chooses, they have to compete on the number for carbohydrates. Of course, none of the other food groups will come close to potatoes and I win the card. A traumatic memory is a top trump card where all the numbers are so high, no other card could possibly beat it.

This means that once you have a traumatic memory, that becomes the sole focus of your subconscious. The other episodic memories still exist, but are cut off by the traumatic memory. Effectively, everything after the traumatic event becomes unsafe. You lose the shades of grey where some things are fine and others require your subconscious to step in. Potentially everything needs your subconscious to step in. This leaves you in a permanent state of high alert. This is not a good state to be in long term, as the physiological changes that kick in when in a state of high alert are only designed for immediate survival. This is why the studies around ACEs demonstrated such a severe long-term impact of childhood trauma. It is also why the focus has been on mitigating the stress effect of those traumatic events. If these traumatic memories are as a result of childhood abuse, then people can be faced with a lifetime of struggling with everything and everyone being unsafe. This is not a good way to live, physically or mentally.

The good news is that, although the database of episodic memories is ignored after trauma, it doesn't actually go away. Those memories still exist, unchanged from the original lessons learned. If you can remove the traumatic element of a traumatic memory, it's like removing the Top Trump card from the pack and you go back to following the other rules.

For trauma, you need to change the way memory is physically stored in that space in the brain. This is not a cognitive, reframing approach. It's just an approach where you mess around with the physical storage of the memory. This is what Eye Movement Desensitisation and Reprocessing (EMDR) does by smudging or blurring it. This is also what the Rewind technique does by moving backwards and forwards through it. In the second section of this book you will find an exercise to help you work on any traumatic memories you may have. With the physical storage of the memory changed, next time your subconscious accesses the database to check if a situation is safe or not, it will find nothing of substance. Without a call to action, you retain cognitive function and can continue without being hijacked. The other advantage of doing this is that, with the traumatic memory effectively removed, you regain access to the episodic memories that allow you to have some structure around your response to different situations. The common factor in both the EMDR and Rewind techniques is the recognition that to change the pain and trauma in a memory, you need to change the way it is physically stored in the brain. Whilst it is not possible to change what happened, it is actually relatively easy to change the meaning in what happened, by changing the dimensions of the memory.

Eye Movement Desensitisation and Reprocessing (EMDR) involves bringing the painful memories forward and using eye movements to change the way the memory is stored. Whilst there is, as yet, no definitive evidence around why it works, there is plenty of information around the different areas used by the brain to store different types of information. It is also recognised that eyes don't see. They are effectively just windows to allow data in, that the brain interprets. EMDR utilises the eyes to move the information around by guiding the person with the traumatic memories to follow a pen or a finger in certain patterns. As we store different things in different parts of the brain, then moving memories around by mixing them up or blurring them, can be very effective. If the storage of a traumatic memory is changed, it can no longer be used as a model for protection.

The other approach that is being used more and more is the Rewind technique. As with EMDR, this technique changes the way the traumatic memory is stored. Instead of using eye patterns, this technique does it by treating the memory as a video clip that is played and re-wound on a repeating cycle, changing the perceptual position of the client as they go forwards and backwards through the memory.

Some people suggest Mindfulness or meditation practices for overcoming trauma, and other issues. Mindfulness has become a mental health buzz word in the last few years. Schools are willing to take on programmes that are labelled with mindfulness or resilience, that they might ignore if labelled with other words such as mental health, mental enhancement or communication skills. Mindfulness has always been out of my reach as a concept. In fact, it used to be just another thing to feel bad about: "You should try mindfulness! It will make you feel calmer and has all sorts of physical benefits" they said. My problem with mindfulness is that it has the wrong name. I think it should be called Body-fulness, as the primary focus appears to be to move away from thoughts and focus on your body. This can lead people, including me, to feel that they are doing a very bad job of being mindful when you can't seem to quieten your thoughts.

Putting that aspect to one side for a moment, the other aspect is to focus on your body and focus on your breathing. This is traditionally approached by sitting still with your eyes closed. There are many people that find stillness relaxing. There are also many people that do not. Often people who have experienced an abusive childhood, or sexual and emotional violence as an adult, find that focussing on the body can have a whole heap of bad associations, triggering an adverse reaction.

I have found, over the years, that instead of trying to relax, a better approach is to learn to accept thoughts, instead of dismissing them. Learn not to allow them to stay long enough in your head to do any damage. The problem is not having the thoughts, it's believing them. At least 90% of the thoughts in your head are what I call 'ninja' thoughts. They are put there by your subconscious and they disguise themselves, so they are indiscernible for the regular, conscious thoughts. How do you know which thoughts you should listen to, and which ones you should ignore? Thoughts, after all, are such a logical and rational thing. They help you decide what to do. They help you know who you are.

If you stand on top of a very tall building, and move towards the edge, your thoughts are going to start yelling at you: "stop or you are going to die". You are going to listen to these thoughts and back off from the edge. Now imagine you are scared of heights and you step onto the bottom rung of a stepladder. Once more your thoughts start yelling at you: "stop or you are going to die". Once more you listen to those thoughts and step back off the stepladder. If you can learn to spot thoughts, and not believe them, then you can have a thought that says "stop or you are going to die", ignore it, and carry on up the stepladder (You probably shouldn't ignore the thought about stepping off the edge of the building!). Most thoughts happen outside of your conscious control, without you even realising it. If you can develop an awareness of your thoughts, then you can begin to bring yourself back into the present, without acting on them.

Moving on from trauma is therefore a two-part process. Firstly, you need to change the way the traumatic memory is stored in the brain, by smudging or blurring it. This will stop it becoming a trigger in your day to day life that takes you out of the present and into a heightened state of anxiety. Once that has been neutralised, then you can work on the meaning in the episodic memories. Remember, you can't time travel. You can't change that traumatic events happened, but you can remove the emotion in them, and thereby change the impact they have on your day to day life.

What purpose does self-harm serve?

Another behaviour that can arise as a result of a difficulty in processing childhood events is self-harm. Have you ever had one of those itches that is deep in your ear canal? They tickle away at you but there is no way you can reach it no matter what you do. Self-harm is a bit like this on a bigger scale. Over the years I tried many things to dampen my thoughts. The level of emotional pain I was experiencing when I was sixteen to eighteen years old was so intolerable that the only way I could get through each moment of each day was to plan how I could kill myself. Crazily, the thought that there was some way I could put an end to it actually made it possible to get though each moment. At that age I didn't have access to alcohol or drugs, and when I tried them at university, I found that it didn't matter how much I drank, I never lost that level of cognitive awareness that I needed to forget how much I hated myself.

One day I started scratching at my arm on the bus on the way to school. I scratched and I scratched, with every intention of making my way down through the skin to my flesh. It was a glorious feeling. It hurt. It was a very real, very visible, very controllable physical pain. I could make it worse. I could make it better. There was an element of punishing myself and deserving the pain, but the main thing I got from it was a real and controllable level of pain. This was not the itch deep in the ear canal that you can't reach. This was not the intense emotional pain that had no physical presence for you or anyone else to see. This was something I could actually see and control. After I had finished scratching, the wound formed a nasty looking scab that was equally as glorious as the original experience of scratching my arm. I could see it. It was there and visible. Others could see it too, if I wanted them to. That wasn't really the point. I didn't really want anyone to see it. If I wanted to, I could pick the scab and I could make it bleed again. I had control over this pain and it felt great. For the next year or so, as well as continually planning how I was going to kill myself, I scratched at my arm. In later years I learnt about how people cut themselves. I hadn't thought of that, but I'm sure if I'd known I would have tried it. I used to regularly dig my fingernails into my flesh until I could see marks that did not disappear when the pressure was removed. As the years went on, the self-harm was less about the controllable pain and more about hating my body and wanting to hurt it. I would visualise slicing the flesh off my stomach. When I went to the dentist, I would imagine using the numbness to slice my face open. I never did any of those things. I had luckily learned, from a fairly young age, not to pay any attention to my thoughts. But it remains my first thought when I am really struggling to cope; I dig my nails into my flesh which brings me back to reality enough to consciously re-engage with far better coping strategies.

Self-harm is similar to the magic button on the wall with addictions. If you find something and it works, why would you not do it when you are struggling to cope? Whilst there is an element of endorphin release in self-harm, the main purpose it serves is to externalise emotional pain into something real and tangible that you can control. Most people who self-harm do it secretly. It is not a call for help. It is an attempt to cope and externalise emotional pain, using something you can directly control.

In this way, anorexia and bulimia are also forms of self-harm. These eating disorders tend to arise from an intense dislike of yourself. This can come from feeling that no one in your peer group likes you, from feeling isolated, from feeling fat and ugly, or feeling that you are a person that no one could ever like. These feelings give rise to attempts to control the only thing you feel you can, your weight. A belief is formed that if you are skinny then people will like you. Soon the control and sense of achievement that you get from controlling your intake, exercising and obsessing over calories, supersedes the original feelings of being not good enough. With other addictive behaviours, there is a feeling of guilt after the fact, when you experience the consequences of your indulgence. With self-harm and eating disorders, there is a sense of satisfaction and control after the behaviour, which makes the desire to let go of the behaviour a lot weaker than with other addictive behaviours. This sense of achievement, combined with the secrecy surround the behaviour, means that you are less likely to seek help than with other screw ups. You are less likely to recognise that you have a problem.

Self-harm puts you in control of things that feel outside of your control. Self-harm can be the sort of problem where friends and family don't find out there is a problem until you are so far down the line with the behaviour, that you are no longer just changing episodic memories and reframing, but you also have to change the behaviour and entire mindset. If you were able to drink as much wine as you wanted or eat as much chocolate as you wanted, with absolutely no consequences, why would you stop? This is the challenge I face when working with those who self-harm or those with anorexia or bulimia. Many recovered anorexia sufferers only made a significant change when they were on death's door. Faced with their own imminent death, for the first time, they saw the true impact of their eating disorder and were able to begin the slow and painful journey to change. Of all the psychological conditions, anorexia has the highest mortality rate, because so many sufferers reach the hospitalised stated before they realise the damage their eating disorder is doing. For many, unfortunately, this realisation comes too late.

So What?

Many years ago, I was delivering a presentation to the CEO of the large company I worked for. The presentation was full of pretty charts and data, demonstrating that my team was getting through more work, and doing it faster. It looked impressive. At the end of the presentation he turned to me and said, "So what?". I stopped in my tracks. He wasn't stupid, and yet after I'd given him all this really cool, and very clear information, asking "so what?", seemed rather flippant. I spluttered an answer, trying to make him see the data again. Then he asked what our customers would say if we asked them how good a job we were doing. In this instance, the call centre management were our customers. I thought for a moment. I realised that he had a valid point. Although we were doing more work, faster, we weren't attending all the critical incidents any faster. In fact, if anything, we were worse at getting to them. Our customers would have presented a very different picture to the one I had just shown to the CEO.

We're all screwed up. That should be clear to you by now. So what? Society is determined to label people as having a mental health problem, or not. Latest research shows that one in four people has a mental health problem. This means that three in four do not. You might have realised from reading this book that it simply cannot be true that only one in four of us is screwed up. I think we need to change the language to "One in four people have a screw up that is getting in the way of their life right now".

If you have a problem with your car, you go and see a mechanic at a garage to fix it.

If you have a problem with a strained muscle, you go and see a Physiotherapist, or a Doctor.

If you have a problem with your head, you assume you should be able to fix it yourself. Why is that? I think it's because of the societal need to diagnose and label. If you go to a doctor with a problem such as exhaustion, a feeling of hopelessness, erratic eating patterns, and other challenges getting through the day, they will need to label you to treat you. You are likely to come out of the appointment knowing you now have depression, armed with some tablets, and possibly an appointment with a counsellor. When you call in to work with your sick line, you tell them you have been signed off with depression. Work is legally required to ensure you are not disadvantaged due to having a mental health condition and will now have to put in place structures and processes to adequately support you. You have stopped being 'Dawn Walton, manager' and have now become a special class of employee with a mental health issue i.e. a disability. If you went to the doctor with a torn muscle, and the first thing they did was to classify you as disabled, and notify everyone to treat you differently, you would probably be less likely to go to the doctor with a torn muscle.

It is not the doctor's fault. They have to treat people for a huge range of issues. Some things are obvious, and other things require them to diagnose. Doctors are as human as the rest of us and will have their own areas of expertise and their own bias. This is often more obvious with weight issues. There are so many differing opinions on what causes issues. The UK introduced a sugar tax so that full sugar drinks cost more. Sugar is regarded as evil and the main reason kids are overweight. In my daughter's school they stopped serving fruit juice because it had too much sugar. Their only option was water or milk. My daughter doesn't like water. Her best friend can't have dairy. I liked my daughter having fruit juice at school. I think it was a healthy thing to do in schools. Because of the sugar tax, and the perception that sugar is bad, this is not possible any more.

Many people have done the Atkins or Keto low carbohydrate diets. The theory behind this is that carbohydrates are fuel for your body, and if you don't burn all the fuel you consume, then the body metabolises the carbohydrates into fat. If you don't put carbohydrates into your body, then it must look elsewhere for fuel, and burns fat. This is called ketosis. This works. However, it puts a huge strain on the kidneys, because it increases the production of acids in the body, called ketones, and one of the functions of the kidneys is to process toxins and acids. I could go on for pages about the different approaches to being healthy, and healthy weight loss. All have some merit and some basis in science. Whichever you have a cognitive bias towards, you will believe in. This is true of medical professionals as well as Joe Bloggs on the street. My daughter's headmistress used to be very pro-sugar tax. She firmly believed that sugar was bad and that children should not eat it. In communicating this, she made my daughter paranoid about her weight in a way she'd never been before. The headmistress made the kids feel unhealthy for wanting sweet treats.

We are born with the ability to listen to our mind body connection. Children will not eat unless they are hungry, and they will not eat until they are so full, they feel sick (unless they have been deprived). It's adults that put rules on what to eat and when. It's adults that teach children to stop listening to their bodies by making them finish everything on their plate, eat at set times, and eat certain combinations of food. People who try and correct being overweight when they are kids, by following some for of externally controlled diet, instead of listening to what their body tells them, tend to struggle with weight for the rest of their lives. If you have started dieting while you were still at school, you are likely to be on some sort of diet for the rest of the life. This is often a situation where you are very aware of what you should be doing, but always falling off the wagon and blowing the diet. Removing the emotional connection to food, and going back to listening to your body is the way to break this cycle.

It is unusual for scientists or medical professionals to look at the mind and body as an entire eco-system. Each will have their own bias, or their own specific area of interest. There are few things that can be looked at in isolation. If you go to the doctor with a perpetual itch in your foot, then the likelihood of finding a solution by looking only at your foot is very slim. You might first look at both feet, and then any other irritations in the skin. You would need to look at blood pressure and circulation, which would lead you to the heart. If you were thorough you may then go on to look at potential stressors for blood pressure being higher, such as diet and environmental stress caused by work, family and friends. To look solely at the foot would dramatically reduce the chances of a permanent solution.

The same approach needs to be true of any issue that appears to originate from the mind. Whilst there is plenty understood about the workings of the body, the mind is still relatively unchartered territory. They are often treated as distinct entities rather than one eco-system. In his book, The Biology of Belief, Bruce Lipton talks of his early days as a lab scientist. His lab supervisor used to constantly tell him "It's the environment, stupid". I always used to think of the nucleus of a cell as the brain of the cell. This probably came from my Biology lessons at school. In his book, Lipton explains that you can kill the nucleus and a cell will continue to 'live' for up to two weeks. However, if you put the cell in a toxic environment, it will die immediately. The membrane of a cell is the main brain of the cell. It communicates changes from the environment, through to the nucleus of the cell, changing its behaviour as necessary.

This cell memory explains how things can be passed between single generations, as opposed to things taking multiple generations to be passed down in the DNA through evolution.

If you paint lines on a road, cattle will know to not walk there, even if they have never been exposed to a cattle grid in their life. It is unlikely that the peril of a cattle grid would be encoded into the DNA, certainly not in the relatively short time since they have been introduced. So how does that knowledge get passed down? My theory is that it is encoded in the cell membrane. This phenomenon has been observed in people. Transgenerational trauma was observed in a 2015 when clinicians observed in 1966 that large numbers of children of Holocaust survivors were seeking treatment in clinics in Canada. The grandchildren of Holocaust survivors were overrepresented by 300% among the referrals to a child psychiatry clinic in comparison with their representation in the general population. This ties in to the studies around ACEs described in the chapter on Addictions, where cells are encoded into a permanently stressed state as a result of adverse experiences in childhood. Whilst more research is needed, in the same way the knowledge of the cattle grid can be passed down, so, it appears, can a heightened level of stress as a result of adverse experiences.

The cells in the body are instructed by the body's eco system. This in turn is regulated by the subconscious. In other words, the brain tells the cells in the body what to do by communicating with the membrane of the cell. The brain is the environments for the cells. If this is ignored then you might work on the cells, but the environment will counter the effects. If you focus only on the presenting symptoms, and ignore the eco system, then you are unlikely to clear any issues permanently. For example, if you treat anxiety about presenting to an audience as only relating to presenting, then you risk missing a deeper level of social anxiety and a fear of being judged, that may hold you back from seeking promotion, or even attending social events. Another example is a client that was in a toxic relationship. We could make changes that allowed them to be okay with themselves, but when they went home after the session, the toxic environment cancelled out those changes. The only way to ensure the changes were permanent was to leave that environment.

If you look at everything, then you might find that someone with irritable bowel syndrome

(IBS) has worse symptoms when they are stressed. You can then look at what causes them to get stressed, and, by removing key stressors, reduce the number of flare ups of the IBS. A doctor might just look at the medical cause of IBS and find that medication and diet does not have the effect they expect.

We need to look at people as an eco-system, with qualities and quirks. Nobody is broken. No matter what your background, you are a fully functioning member of society. You must be, as you are reading this book! You have your screw ups. That is normal and perfectly okay. The only time they are not okay, is when your life is being limited by them. When that happens, you should get some help to sort it.

I hope, as you've read this book, that you've realised that you are actually relatively normal. I often feel I need to apologise when I call my clients normal. It seems like such an insult! More than anything, I would like you to finish reading this book and realise that change is always possible. You probably are screwed up, we all are. It may be true that you have functioned perfectly well throughout your life, despite your screw ups. If you are happy right now, then nothing needs to change. Go ahead and live your life, realising that all around you are screwed up people doing exactly that. If, however, your screw up is getting in the way of you living your life at the moment, then realise it doesn't have to be that way. Change is always possible, just not necessarily easy!

Part 2 – Self-Help Toolkit

When I wrote my first book, The Caveman Rules of Survival, I wrote it as an insight into the way the brain works using a primitive rule set from the caveman days. I was surprised to find that many people used it as a self-help book. Although I included tips at the end of each chapter, it was not designed as a book to help people overcome their issues, more to be aware of them.

However, it did teach me that if you trigger memories, and your writing resonates, then it's important to make sure that you give people something to use, rather than just leave you making it up for yourself!

Therefore, with this book I have created this section of tools and techniques that you can apply, should you wish to, to work through some of the issues that may have resonated as you read this book.

It is not designed as a replacement for expert help. It is designed to allow you to see how easy it can be to change issues that you have been struggling with your whole life. Maybe some of these techniques will be enough. Maybe not. The main thing I would like you to take away is that change is possible. Try some of the techniques. Notice what change is possible,

We're all screwed up (and that's ok)

then, once you realise that, go and get some expert help.

Learning not to believe thoughts

This exercise is designed to help you learn how to spot thoughts, allow them in, and then send them away again, before you have a chance to believe them and act on them. During this exercise you are merely learning a skill. You are not acting on it.

Part 1: 60 seconds a day.

The goal of this first step is to spot, allow in, and move on, every single thought that enters your head for a period of 60 seconds. Every single thought. If it's a critical item on your to-do list, move it on. If it's the best idea you have ever had in your life, move it on. If it's something you are really worried about, move it on. This exercise is simply about learning to recognise every thought that enters your head, and choose what to do with them. It is working with temporary brain space. Anything important will remain in permanent storage so there is no need to worry.

As thoughts are quite abstract, we first need to learn how to turn the thoughts into objects. The most common object my clients choose is a bubble. A bubble is easy to visualise because it can disappear easily when you pop it. I also have people that choose the "swipe right or left" approach you can use on certain devices. It doesn't matter what your visualisation is as long as you follow two simple rules:

1. Every thought must turn into exactly the same object. You are not analysing, categorising your thoughts. You are simple saying "oh, there is a thought" for every single thought that enters your head.
2. Whatever you do with the object, it must fully disappear. This is why the bubble is such a popular option. Throwing thoughts away isn't going to fully get rid of them. They will build up in a pile wherever you throw them. As the goal is to fully dismiss thoughts, this is not going to meet the objective of this task.

For 60 seconds, every day for a week, all you do is notice each thought, turn it into an object, and get rid of it. Don't do anything else at the same time. You are using the 60 seconds to master the skill, not to actually execute on it.

Part 2: Week 2 – 2 minutes.

After a week, if you find that you can get through the whole 60 seconds without checking your timer all the time, then you can increase the time to 2 minutes for the next week. However, if you are struggling to get through the 60 seconds, keep going until you can do a whole 60 seconds without checking the timer, then up it to 2 minutes.

Once you can successfully complete this exercise for a whole two minutes, you are effectively a Zen master and you won't need to do it anymore.

As you master the skill of identifying and dismissing thoughts, you may find that the skill begins to creep into your day to day life. You can become aware of damaging or limiting thoughts, and with that awareness comes the ability to dismiss the thoughts. Consider a scenario where you are at work and one of your colleagues seems a bit cool in their response when you greet them in the corridor. You immediately begin to wonder what you have done to make them respond to you in that way. You dig through your memories to try and work it out and decided that they must be unhappy that you have not yet done that report you promised them. It's annoying because you have had loads of work to do and you've just not had time to work on that report yet. It seems a little unfair that they are having a go at you. After all, if they'd just asked you would have explained that you were swamped right now. There was absolutely no call for them to treat you that way. Next time you see that co-worker, you are really snappy with them. The problem is, the cool look was probably just because they were thinking about something else. Maybe someone had said something to them and they were worried about it, or maybe they were just thinking about what to do for dinner that night. You have no idea because you can't read their mind. If you had enough of an awareness of your thoughts you could spot the very first thought "I wonder why they are being to off with me" and dismiss it, before it stayed in your head and lead to all the other thoughts, and ultimately a change in your behaviour.

This skill, in time, can become a bit like a super power; you are human so are still going to get screwed up by stuff, but the time it takes you to get over it gets shorter and shorter as you stop believing the lies your head is telling you.

Using the thoughts exercise before sleep

Unlike when you use this as a daily exercise, at night time, as you dismiss your thoughts, you should do it without any sort of timer on it. I can guarantee that this is more effective than counting sheep! Every time a thought enters your head, turn it into an object and dismiss it. You can remain in your semi-conscious state. As you have already sorted through the thoughts, when you enter your REM sleep cycle your subconscious already knows where things go. This results in a natural two-hour REM cycle, a natural six-hour restorative cycle, leaving you refreshed the next day. As your batteries are fully recharged, it becomes easier to process the daily events, meaning the night time thought exercise is also easier.

Logging your positives

This is how the neural pathways in your brain work. Each time you travel a pathway by having a particular thought or practicing a particular skill, that pathway in your brain is thickened, making it easier to travel in the future. Whenever a neural pathway is ignored, it gets thinner and eventually disappears.

As your brain is constantly being updated, and overwriting what was there previously, it is a relatively simple process to build these new pathways, you just have to choose to do it. This takes us back to the whole idea of "don't think of a pink elephant". If you deliberately notice something, it means you travel a neural pathway. If you then write that thing down, due to reconsolidation theory, that piece of information is added to the list for processing while you sleep. It adds it to the brain 'to-do' list. Each time you actively and deliberately notice something, by writing it down or verbalising it with someone else, you add to the memory and the pathway. Simply thinking it does little to enhance the pathway as you have millions of thoughts.

> • At the end of each day with three positive things that have happened in your day. These do not have to be big things. They can be small things like "I had a smile from the person on the till at the supermarket" or they can be big things like "applied for the job I wanted".

What is important, when writing an evidence log, is to only write those things you want to remember in your day. Ask yourself "Of all the paths I travelled today, which one do I want to travel easily again in the future" and that's what you write down.

The mistake many people make is they write these daily positives in a "I did this but..." way.

For example: "I applied for the job I want, even though I don't think I've any chance of getting it". If we split this statement into two paths:

1. I applied for the job I wanted (Positive)
2. I don't think I've any chance of getting it (Negative)

You can see there is a mixed message for the brain here. It may well create and reinforce the path about applying for the job. But it will also reinforce the path for the belief that you can't get the job. As we are naturally in a protective negative path most of the time, that path is likely to already exist and be much thicker than the positive path. By writing down that statement in that way, you effectively negate the value of the positive statement because it will still be overridden by the negative part. What is important is to only write down the first part and leave the second as just a thought that will not get locked in during the sleep cycle.

1. Felt calmer about asking for help
2. Chose to ask for help
3. Felt confident about asking where something was.

In this way you are building neural pathways to the things that you want your brain to recognise and reward you for in the future.

Overriding emotional hijacking

In this exercise I am going to take you through creating a happy anchor, but the steps are the same for any positive emotion. Maybe calm/relaxed works better for you, or excited, or proud, or confident. Just follow these steps with your selected emotion.

1. Select a positive emotion that you want to be able to instantly invoke – for this example, "happy".
2. Allow your mind to wander back in time until you find an example of feeling happy. It doesn't have to be a massive event. It can be something as simple like taking a walk in the sunshine, or your child giggling, or the first sip of a really nice cup of coffee. If you can't think of anything, then try a different emotion like confident. I am sure there is something in your life that you can feel confident doing. Even something simple like making a cup of tea, or tying your shoelaces, is good enough.
3. With that memory in mind I want you to focus on that happy feeling. If that was somewhere inside your body, where would it be?

> 4. If that happy feeling had a colour, what would the colour be?
> 5. If that colour was in some sort of shape, what shape would it be? Is that a 3D or a 2D shape?
> 6. Does that colour/shape move? Or maybe it has a temperature?

Now we need to understand your anchor a little more.

> 1. If you were to feel less happy (let's assume that's sad) what would happen to the colour, size and movement of the anchor?
> 2. If you were to feel more happy, what would happen to the colour, size and movement of the anchor?
> 3. Make the anchor more and more happy, channelling the happiness into that shape.

Next, I want you to imagine storing that anchor in your head. You should try and find a small object that is similar in colour (if not shape) to the anchor you just created. It should be small enough to carry around with you or have on your desk. It should NOT be an item of clothing. If you have the anchor with you and visible at all times, then it will dilute the effect when you call on it to counter a negative emotion. The different between the positive anchored state and the negative emotional state will not be noticeable enough.

Next time you feel a negative emotion that you need to move on from, either look at the object or just imagine taking the anchor from within your head. It will cancel out the negative emotion, returning your thinking brain to you, and allowing you to think rationally again.

The other thing you can do with an anchor is stack it. Next time you feel a positive emotion that even remotely resembles the one you have anchored, you can imagine zapping it in to your anchored object, making it even more powerful for you next time you need it.

'Use' your anchor by recalling it any time you become aware of emotional switch off.

Clearing episodic memories using reframing.

As discussed in previous chapters, it's not what happens that causes you a problem. It's the incorrect meaning attached to memories, which are then stored and act as triggers. It is episodic memories, not autobiographical ones that cause the real problems.

This means that if you can change the way a memory is stored, then you can change the meaning. If a memory loses its meaning, it will not trigger the subconscious to switch the cognitive functions off, to take you into a protective state.

Firstly, I want to demonstrate how easy it is to change the way the brain is triggered.

Skip steps 1-4 if you don't want to develop an aversion to a food type! Seriously. Don't even read them.

1. I want you to think of a single item of food that you would like to stop eating. Make sure you pick something that you really don't want to eat any more. Make sure it's not something like onions or tomatoes i.e. something that is in many dishes. It's best to choose

something like a particular chocolate bar, or snack. Be very specific.

2. Next, I want you to think of a food you absolutely hate. Something where the smell, texture or taste almost makes you gag. If you have not got that, then think of a disgusting bodily fluid like sick, urine or...you know...use your imagination.

3. Now I want you to imagine taking a bite of the food you would like to stop eating. As you bring it closer to your mouth, imagine it is covered in whatever you thought up in step 2. As it gets closer to your mouth the smell and texture become clearer and stronger. Imagine opening your mouth and starting to get the disgusting taste of the horrible thing on your tongue.

4. As you move the item of food away, notice how the sensations diminish. Keep doing that until even just holding that food type invokes the disgusting reaction.

Your brain has been updated with a different association with that food type that you picked, just using your imagination.

All it takes to permanently change the way a memory is stored is a little imagination. Because you can't un-see or un-think something, then any change in the way you see something will update the memory. If the memory has changed, the meaning has to change. Maybe, when you were a child, you did those puzzles where you had to follow a number of paths through a maze to find the right one that connected the start and finish. Maybe it was connecting a kitten to a ball of string, or a football to a goal. Depending on how complicated the structure of the maze was, you could either do this by eye, or follow along the different paths with a pen until you got it right.

Example 1: A simple example – a worm and an apple

In my childhood story of the apple and the worm, I could imagine that the worm changed into a jelly worm.

I could bite in and notice a lovely, colourful jelly worm. I could think myself lucky that I found a sweet in my apple. This is quite easy for me to do because it's not an intensely emotional memory. I have enough of my cognitive function still engaged to be able to reframe and change the dimensions of the memory into something more appealing using my imagination.

Example 1: A more complex example – worrying what people think of you

1. If you were to stand in front of a room full of people, or go into a social situation with lots of strangers, how would you feel?

2. Why would you feel that way? What's the worst thing that could happen? (e.g. I'd be embarrassed, they'd laugh at me, they'd realise I didn't know what I was talking about)

3. Thinking about the emotion in step 2, if that was somewhere in your body where would it be?

4. If you were to treat this as a part of you, what would you call it (trust me when I say to go with whatever pops to mind no matter how weird!)

5. Thinking of this part, what is it protecting you from? What is its intent? (it may help to think of what would happen if it wasn't there). It is always a positive intent, so if you are thinking of something negative, keep trying!

6. If you were to think back to when you were first aware of this part of you, would it be before you were 5, between 5 and 10 or after you were 10? Really go back and see if it was there at each age.

7. Now imagine you are a fly on the wall at this earliest point in time, looking down at the younger you, what would you notice about how you the younger you is feeling?

8. Surround this younger version of you in something that allows them to see, but not be seen. A bubble is good, an invisibility cloak or a blanket can also be really useful. Or something else entirely. What did you use? What colour was it (if applicable)?

9. Now for the really tricky bit. We need you to change something about that memory. Within that safe place, notice something about the other people that you didn't originally notice. Write down what the memory was and what you changed

- Remember you can't read minds

- Remember we are all screwed up.

- Remember that whatever is happening, you will be fine. You will be here, doing this exercise

10. Add that better feeling to the thing you created in step 8

Clearing Traumatic memories

Memories that hold more emotion and traumatic memories cannot be cognitively reframed, as you are unlikely to retain enough cognitive function when immersed in the associated intense emotions. **Please be aware, some memories are too traumatic for you to attempt any work on them on your own. Seek professional support for these memories.**

None of these are likely to feel like you have made a significant change. However, there will be a difference in your emotional response over time. We are not changing that it happened. We can't change time. We are changing what it meant. For traumatic and painful memories, try one or more of the following:

- Zoom in and out, like a psychedelic disco.
- Change it from blurry to sharp and back
- Make it greyscale, or if it already is, make it colourful. Saturate and intensify the colours
- Imagine a music track that is fun and upbeat and imagine playing it while thinking of the memory. Turn the volume up to maximum.

> - Change the speed of the memory. Rewind it fast and play it forward really slowly.
> - If there is a person involved, change their voice to something ridiculous like they've breathed in a helium balloon, or Donald Duck. If their voice sounds ridiculous, it makes what they are saying ridiculous. Your brain only learns from stuff that hurts you, not ridiculous things.

Any one of those approaches will fundamentally change the storage of the memory. This change will lose the connections that allow your subconscious to refer to it.

ABOUT THE AUTHOR

Dawn C. Walton was born in North Wales in 1972. She is a happily married mother of one girl and is a full time Cognitive Hypnotherapist and public speaker, with a practice based in Scotland. She also helps people all over with an online therapy model.

She is passionate about helping people realise that we are all screwed up, and uses her experiences of an abusive childhood to help others find peace and happiness.

You can get in touch through her website at www.thinkitchangeit.com or on Facebook by searching for Think it Change it.

30894220R00151

Printed in Great
Britain
by Amazon